BLACK PIONEERS

BLACK

Images of the Black Experience on the North American Frontier

PIONEERS

Second Edition

JOHN W. RAVAGE

Foreword by Quintard Taylor

THE UNIVERSITY OF UTAH PRESS
Salt Lake City

The Defiance House Man colophon is a registered trademark of the
University of Utah Press. It is based upon a four-foot-tall, Ancient
Puebloan pictograph (late PIII) near Glen Canyon, Utah.

13 12 11 10 09   1 2 3 4 5

LIBRARY OF CONGRESS CATALOGING-IN-PUBLICATION DATA

Ravage, John W., 1937-
  Black pioneers : images of the Black experience on the North American frontier /
John W. Ravage ; foreword by Quintard Taylor. — 2nd ed.
      p. cm.
  Includes bibliographical references.
  ISBN 978-0-87480-941-1 (pbk. : alk. paper) 1. African American pioneers—West
(U.S.)—History—Pictorial works. 2. Frontier and pioneer life—West (U.S.)—Picto-
rial works. 3. West (U.S.)—History—Pictorial works. I. Title.
  E185.925.R38 2009
  978'.00496073—dc22

                          2008041471

Cover photo courtesy of the Lewis County Historical Museum, Chehalis, Washington.

Unless otherwise noted, all images are courtesy of the author.

Printed and bound by Sheridan Books, Inc., Ann Arbor, Michigan.

For Chris, Jeff, Amanda, Emma, Ian, and

Elias, of whom I am immensely proud,

and as a partial answer to the actor, William Marshall,

who asked me some forty years ago, "And what are you

doing about racial issues in our society?"

Contents

Foreword

PICTURES TELL A POWERFUL STORY. They can alter the way we look at the world and determine the manner in which our history is imagined. John W. Ravage, professor emeritus of the University of Wyoming and the author of *Black Pioneers,* proves this adage in persuasive and often ironic ways. With a focus on African Americans in the American West, the region of the United States least identified with black history, Ravage has searched private and public collections in every western state as well as provincial archives in Canada to assemble more than three hundred rare photographs, lithographs, daguerreotypes, line drawings, block prints, sketches, and other images to tell a story of black inclusion in the region's past. Ravage is careful to present his images and accompanying text not as analytical or narrative history, but his volume nonetheless cannot help but buttress the claims of a growing number of western historians that the region's saga remains incomplete without the stories of black westerners.

Expanding on the work he released a decade ago, this new edition contains expanded chapters on entertainers and artists and on African American photographers such as Galveston's Lucius Harper, Denver's John Green, and the peripatetic James P. Ball of Helena, Seattle, and Honolulu, among other places, all of whom helped compile a photographic record that provides an amazing glimpse into black western life. This volume also includes new images of black settlers drawn from little-known collections in archives and personal papers such as the Stepp Family Ranch Papers in Wyoming, as well as the records of communities such as Dearfield, Colorado, and Cat Creek, Wyoming. With the additional materials, this second edition of *Black Pioneers* is almost twice as large as the original volume.

Black Pioneers includes images of the famous, such as an 1867 French drawing of fur trapper and mountain man James Beckworth, or the first authentic twentieth-century black cowboy movie hero, Herb Jeffries. Those images are to be expected. What is surprising is the range of images of ordinary African Americans—barbers in Denver, teachers in Hawaii, loggers in Idaho, ranchers in Nevada, homesteaders in Alberta, midwives in Colorado, and sailors and ship captains in Alaska. Although most of the images are from the nineteenth century, the inclusion of third-generation South Dakota businessman Ted Blakey (with Ronald Reagan) at the 1980 Republican National Convention is a reminder of the number of twenti-eth- and twenty-first-century descendants of the early pioneers.

Our image of black westerners is repeatedly challenged by the photo-graphs of people such as R. J. von Dickersohm, a Zulu chief and veteran of the 1879 Battle of Isandala in South Africa where the British Twenty-fourth Infantry was annihilated. Von Dickersohm, fearing British retalia-tion, moved first to Germany and then to Denver, where he died in 1940.

Ravage's remarkable photos assembled in *Black Pioneers* answer the questions distinguished actor William Marshall posed to him more than three decades ago, "And what are you doing about race issues in our soci-ety?" His answer is evident in this volume. Through hundreds of images Ravage is recrafting and recasting the image of African Americans in the West to remind us that black history is all around us, touching every cor-ner of the United States.

— Quintard Taylor

Preface

A DECADE HAS PASSED since the first edition of this work, and I find that most of my earlier observations about the roles of African Americans in the North American West still apply. What has changed significantly, however, is the breadth, depth, and candor of studies from an increasing number of scholars about those roles. In 2009 we find that nearly all colleges and universities offer courses focusing on the achievements of blacks and their place in American history. Though still in its early stages, the search for fair and balanced presentations of African American history is expanding rapidly. The goal of this second edition is to offer a fresh pictorial perspective to this growing body of scholarship.

After the Civil War, profound changes took place in the living patterns of African Americans. While most of the newly freed black men and women chose to remain in the South, some migrated north, seeking employment and other opportunities. A small but significant number of these black adventurers, however, moved to the American and Canadian West.

A romanticized story of the post–Civil War movement of people to the West has long been depicted in literature, films, and other popular entertainment. The mythical American West is filled with strong and often heroic men and women—the sons and daughters of stout European forebears. Not surprisingly, the role played by African Americans and other minority groups in the history of the West has largely been ignored.

The purpose of this book is to reveal how black contributions to western history have been overlooked. Through photographs and other graphic images of black pioneers and their work and experiences, their historical presence is revealed. Through pictures, we find black laborers, professionals, builders, gamblers, roughnecks, politicians, leaders, followers—good men and women, bad ones too—with the stamina and drive required to face hostile environments, hoping to build a secure future.

The man in this photograph, described as "Chief of the Shirashep," is actually
Clifford Hancock, a civilian employee of the U.S. military dressed as
a fanciful "black Eskimo." Taken in Alaska in 1899, this image is an indication
of the increasing influence of African Americans in that northern region.

(Courtesy of the Rasmussen Collection, University of Alaska Archives, Fairbanks.)

The presence of black Americans in the West is not widely documented. Thus, it comes as no surprise that the general perception was
that they were so few in number as to have played an inconsequential role
in developing that vast region. Based on 1870 and 1880 population statis-
tics, however, it is now clear that African Americans constituted approximately 1.5 to 3 percent of nineteenth-century settlers in the West, numbering as many as 150,000 souls. Assuming that a large percentage of them
were employed as laborers, it is likely that some 15,000 to 20,000 were entrepreneurs and professionals engaged in various endeavors in both small
and large communities.[1] These numbers are significant, given the sparse
settlement patterns of the era. It may thus be supposed that their influence
on western development was far more significant than is generally cred-

The racism implicit in both early advertising and motion pictures is
displayed in this "intermission slide" from Grand Island, Nebraska, circa 1905.
Audiences were barraged with this kind of imagery.

(Courtesy of the American Heritage Center, University of Wyoming, Laramie.)

ited. What western North America has become is derived in part from the
cultural vitality of its African American settlers.

This text contains approximately three hundred illustrations that call
unaccustomed attention to a period in American history that has been ne-
glected by the narrow vision of a relatively few writers—and a large number of historians. My intention has been to collect images and profiles of
the rich and poor, good and bad, young and old, men and women, so that
part of the record of those earlier times might document that the residents of western North America and Alaska were truly a tumbled mix of
racial heritages, philosophies, and accomplishments. Here, then, are the
pictures and stories of black pioneers who changed the face of our continent forever.

Although the bulk of the illustrations are photographs, many are
in other forms, including lithographs, line drawings, block prints, and
sketches. These pictorial representations—found in the mass media of
the era—were the sole means by which predominantly white audiences
formed their ideas of not only how black men and women looked but also
how they fitted into the contemporary historical and political realities.

In searching for every conceivable kind of image in newspapers, books, and periodicals, I started with the period of heaviest migration, approximately 1865, and stopped my search near the end of the "cattle kingdom" era in the West, circa 1920. It was during this period that eastern readers and European audiences came to understand the scope of the country's Manifest Destiny and watched with excitement as pioneers forged their way across the frontier, headed toward the Pacific. These readers saw few depictions of pioneer African American men and women, however, even though they constituted a substantial minority of the settlers moving west of the Mississippi River as well as into western Canada and Alaska. Then, as now, we were a nation that concentrated overmuch on the contributions of the "majorities" in our midst and downplayed those of "minorities." But attitudes can change in the presence of new insights.

I have included not only items seldom found in print but also those that—though perhaps more commonly seen—are the only known images of some individuals. Many of the illustrations that follow exist in no other printed form or in publications with a small circulation. But to leave out the more familiar representations would create an incomplete and misleading record. Overall, the images present a fresh look at the roles played by African Africans in the western United States, Canada, and Alaska in the period of greatest expansion.

In order to research and assemble all of the material, I have traveled to and examined more than one hundred collections and corresponded with curators of at least fifty others. Since the publication of the first edition, two dozen or more archives have gone out of existence, their collections often absorbed by larger institutions with more secure footing. Although I found much of the material in archives ranging from small museum and library collections to major holdings in state, provincial, and educational institutions, other valuable sources were in private collections, scattered in out-of-the-way places (see the List of Collections).

As might be expected, the quality of hundred-year-old photographs varies widely. Master negatives were seldom available, except in government repositories, and often those archives possessed only copies of originals. Other than cleaning and rephotographing with high-quality modern film, few attempts were made to restore the images. Though a strong argument could be made for enhancement through digitizing or other electronic means—indeed, this might make some pictures clearer—the majority appear here in their original form. Only in those few cases where an image seemed extremely important to the text but was virtually unusable were other means employed to copy the prints.

Minor obstacles to research sometimes arose because matters involving race still elicit strong emotions and are often barriers to collecting information about blacks and other minority ethnic groups. However, most curators and archivists were eager to advance the cause of this expanded view of the place of African Americans in western history.

Although this book has never been intended to be the seminal work on the subject, neither is it devoted solely to prominent African Americans. Instead, I have strived to display a cross-section of the wide range of individuals who came to live and work in places often regarded as remote or insignificant. I aim to demonstrate that these individuals were builders of permanent residences for themselves and their families in an area stretching from the edge of Illinois to the shores of the Pacific, from Mexico to the Arctic Circle. Their contributions to the settlement of the American West have gone largely unacknowledged for far too long.

I have made no attempt to cover every western state, territory, province, or municipality. Instead, my intention is to describe the widespread settlement of African Americans in western areas of the continent, as well as those places where the western mystique was promulgated and popularized. It will be up to other researchers to flesh out the details, and I hope additional studies will be forthcoming that will accurately examine the particulars.

I have been collecting images of African Americans—primarily photographs and primarily from the West—for nearly thirty-five years and have amassed a sizable inventory, only a fraction of which is represented here. The desire to show the broadest possible range has informed my choices. In this second edition, I have included more information regarding the dates of images and clues to occupations and social positions, as a way to assist those who have personal collections to research.

I am not a historian, nor do I pretend to be. My interest in this endeavor derives from my background as a professor of media with a special interest in photographic images. I am more interested in verifying the existence of these individuals and less interested in a historical analysis of their contributions or importance. As media, photographs become part of a communications network; they are the precursors of television and motion pictures and what eventually came to be described as "mass media." All these more modern developments have massively reconstructed our understanding of American history and the contributions of ethnic groups to our development as a country.

James Beckworth (sometimes Beckwith or Beckwourth) was a gambler, explorer, and entrepreneur who traversed the mountains and plains of Montana, Wyoming, California, Colorado, and Nevada. This halftone image from a French magazine of the times indicates that his popularity extended far beyond America's boundaries and stimulated the imaginations of Europeans about all things related to the American West, especially roles of black men and women.

(Courtesy of the American Heritage Center, University of Wyoming, Laramie.)

John James Audubon, as depicted in his *Birds of America*. The son of a married French sea captain and a Haitian woman, he inherited the aquiline features of his father and the skin tones—not depicted here—of his mother.

(Courtesy of the White House Collection, Washington, D.C.)

1800s Photography

The popularity of photography in the mid- to late 1800s and early 1900s was a powerful addition to the growing acceptance, rightly or wrongly, of mass media as the recorders of truth. Therefore, the images that history has left us of pioneers of all colors strongly influence how we view the "place" of African Americans in our country's earlier years.

Stories of ex-slave mountain men and others of both great and ordinary achievement have been nearly lost. However, those figures were some of the "images" presented to other Americans—images upon which many of the concepts of social roles, such as racial stereotyping, were based. In their own way, these stereotypic images affected the cultural heritage of the Western world and not solely the residents of the United States. Contained in these images were implied standards for what was deemed respectable, acceptable, and useful for black men and women in our society. These concepts were limiting factors for many of the pioneers and their descendants. But when viewed over history's shoulder, they also show how many of these men and women began to break the shackles that time and society had placed on them as they moved into new lands and dared new experiences.

It is unfortunate that inaccurate accounts have long influenced public perceptions about the historical role that blacks played in the making of the West. To cite two egregious examples: African American explorer, mountain man, and Crow Indian war chief James "Jim" Beckworth was once portrayed by the white actor Jack Oakie (whose real name was Lewis Delaney Offield and who, not incidentally, was a well-known pratfall comedian of the 1930s, '40s, and '50s) in the 1951 film *Tomahawk*. Likewise, when American artist John Syme painted a portrait of John James Audubon in 1826, he depicted this mixed-race native of Haiti as a white man.

There is, obviously, no way to change the past; the best we can often do is understand events in light of a growing base of knowledge and modern attitudes and perceptions. This process depends more on what we know about ourselves at any given time than on what we know about the past.

Acknowledgments

I CONTINUE TO BE INDEBTED to substantial research aid from the University of Wyoming's Department of Communication and Mass Media (and unremitting support from chair Frank Millar) as well as Michael Devine and Richard Ewig of the American Heritage Center at the University of Wyoming and a research grant from the University of Wyoming. Special appreciation is extended to Melinda Bobo and many unnamed others for their skills in copyediting, proofing, and indexing.

Most important, the constant support of my wife, Linda Ravage, made the project achievable and enjoyable. She has endured two decades of traveling to collections; browsing in museums; scouring flea markets, sales, and auctions; and has given constant attention to details that I overlook with great frequency.

BLACK PIONEERS

❀ 1 ❀

Moving Westward and Northward

Good God! may the time come when thou shall stretch out thy strong
arm, and say to his mighty deluge, which is sweeping myriads and
myriads to enthraldom and a degraded servitude, who are entitled
to equal rights and privileges with ourselves, hitherto shalt thou
come, and no further, and here shall thou proud waves be stayed!

— Quoted in George Washington Ogden,
"Letters from the West" (1821)

IN THE DECADES FOLLOWING the American Civil War, the vast majority of African Americans remained in the South, perhaps out of a sense of familiarity or obligation, if nothing else. Most had little choice but to remain where they were; being poor, they lacked the means and resources to go anywhere else. Some brave individuals chanced a better future and moved to the North in search of better-paying jobs. A few, however, were pulled into the western migration that swept the country after the war.

The Old West was a dynamic place. There was gold rushing in California, British Columbia, and the Yukon; cattle ranching in Texas, New Mexico, and Indian Territory (Oklahoma); and railroad construction across the Great Plains. There were mountains and passes waiting to be explored and "conquered" by men and women courageous or foolhardy enough to try. It seemed that opportunities abounded for those with able minds and bodies, and thousands of former slaves took advantage, striving to grab their share of the American dream.

Most of these black adventurers followed the railroad, which was then beginning to connect areas with the rest of the country; the transcontinental railroad became a reality in May 1869. Some of the earliest job opportunities available to these new emigrants were on the trains as porters, butchers, waiters, cooks, service personnel, loaders, and baggage clerks.

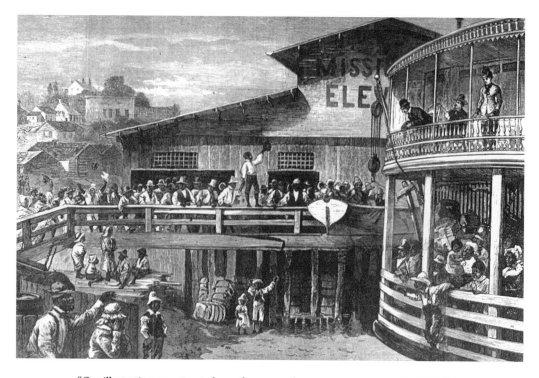

"Our illustration on page 284 has reference to the great movement now being made by the Negro race from their accustomed homes in the South to the more tranquil region west of the Mississippi. Fugitives from injustice and oppression, these people are fleeing northward and westward, as others of their race previously fled from the horrors of slavery. Deprived of their own civil rights, they are now in their own section of our country, nearly as far from the enjoyment of the privileges granted them by the Constitution as they were in their day of bondage." (*Harper's Weekly*, May 17, 1879.)

They filled almost any but the "front-end" positions, which, of course, were held by whites—engineers, firemen, and station clerks. Ultimately, the job of conductor became almost the sole domain of those black men fortunate enough to remain employed long enough by the railroad.

There were other jobs to be had and black men and women willing to take them as well. Many of these job hunters stopped and stayed along the train routes, creating niches in the growing economies of the small towns that sprang up to meet the demands of the railroads. By 1900, for example, the overwhelming majority of barbers in the country were African American, a fact often overlooked by historians and other scholars.

The way west for these newly relocated citizens was inextricably mixed with the movement of others also searching for personal success.

Punishing slaves as examples to others occurred with regularity and great brutality.
This engraving, from England, shows a master disciplining with a cricket bat.

Immigrant Irish, Chinese, English, Scottish, Scandinavian, German, and Russian workers were part of an influx of newcomers that would peak within fifty years.

As opportunities for employment began to stratify, entrepreneurs and hustlers dominated the economic life of the new cities and towns; unskilled laborers were forced to gravitate toward labor-intensive positions, like working cattle or heavy industrial jobs; women were less likely to find employment as a result of social stereotyping, and they were primarily untrained workers to begin with. Blacks, Chinese, Japanese, Indians, and mixed-race individuals stood at the bottom of the job ladder, forced to take whatever was left over.

Or so it seemed to historians of the early twentieth century as they looked back on those times. As with all such generalizations, there were many and varied exceptions. At the start of the twenty-first century, we are only beginning to realize the full range of activities in which black pioneers were engaged. The popular media have long compounded our ignorance about the black past by producing stories about heroes who either

A conductor and workers with their white colleagues on the Union Pacific Railroad stationed in Laramie, Wyoming, circa 1890. To most railway travelers of the era, service jobs like these were the only ones they associated with African Americans.

never existed or were dramatically modified to appeal to the sentiments of newspapers and pulp fiction readers, motion picture audiences, and—more recently—television viewers.

As perspectives became distorted, it was nearly impossible to separate fact from fiction. The contributions of blacks and other racial and ethnic minorities became less and less prevalent in history texts and in popular entertainment. Nonwhites ceased to exist, essentially, in many aspects of our nation's history.

In actuality, however, African Americans played the same role in the development of western North America as did whites and other ethnic groups. They fought and died, raised children, killed and were killed, smuggled, lied, womanized, and drank to excess; they were God-loving and God-fearing, lawmen and outlaws, mountaineers and townspeople, millionaires and paupers; they built cities and towns and destroyed them, too; they fought Indians and protected travelers, just as whites did.

Auction of slaves in Texas, lithograph, circa 1860. Although there were
images of individuals in service occupations, more drawings of them
as slaves at auction appeared in the media of the day.
(Courtesy of the Institute for Texan Cultures, San Antonio.)

Black men and women were assigned, in the spirit of the times, to relatively insignificant places in society. They could hold menial jobs without offending the far more numerous whites who dominated most cities
and towns. In this environment, human individuality mutated into stereotypic "facts," as servants, laborers, dissemblers, and shufflers were invariably interpreted in newspapers, novels, stage plays, and, later, films and
television.

In reality, however, former slaves and their progeny were spending
their days and nights much the same as white and other ethnic newcomers to the West. For every white con man, there was a black one; for every
Asian laundryman, there was a black one—and a white one, for that matter. Life was as complex for people then as it is now, and those who experienced it were just as hard-pressed to succeed as are many of their descendants today.

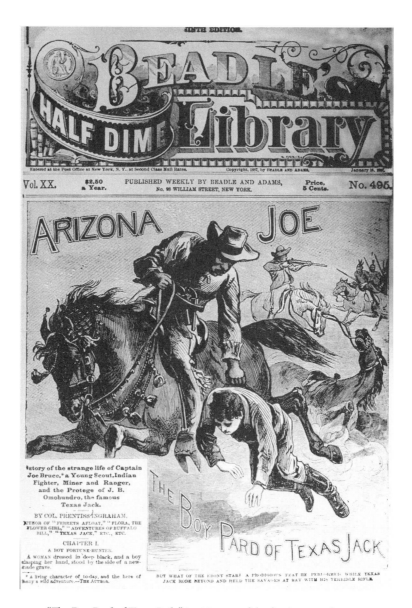

"The Boy Pard of Texas Jack," in 1887, one of the few images of a penny dreadful's black hero to survive from the past. Although he was the "sidekick" of the protagonist, he did gain top billing on the cover.

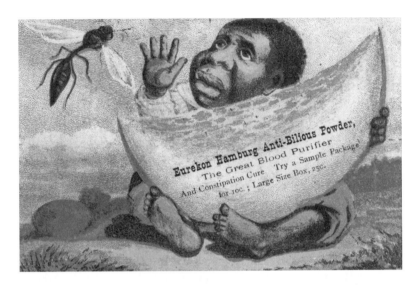

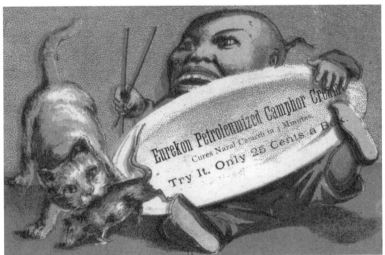

Advertising cards from the 1880s. Often, differing racial stereotypes were inserted with identical advertising copy on each. The intent was to reinforce popular beliefs about a person's appearance and social worth.

THE WEST

*The West, at bottom, is a form of society, rather than
an area. It is the term applied to the region whose social
conditions result from the application of older institutions
and ideas to the transforming influences of free land.*

— Frederick Jackson Turner,
The Frontier in American History (1929)

North America was, in many ways, segmented in its attractiveness to emigrants, especially those recently freed from slavery. The trans-Mississippi West lured some who sought to leave the Old South to find success and prosperity; their presence in northern and eastern parts of the United States and Canada dates from the seventeenth century.

Stereotypes always seemed to accompany newcomers to areas populated with large numbers of settlers. If the South had myths based on appearance, religion, skin color, and educational levels, so did the West. In colonial times, for example, areas west of New York and Philadelphia were "terra incognita," and Canada was a haven for traitors, rascals, royalists, and runaways, as far as many residents of the original thirteen colonies were concerned.

By the early nineteenth century, Indiana, Kentucky, and Tennessee were the outermost reaches of American expansion. By midcentury, large-scale migration west and north across the Great Plains had changed the lines once again. The trans-Mississippi West had become a relatively concise designation for "the West" in 1819 with the construction of Fort Atkinson to protect traffic on the Missouri River. Consistent with the military's mission to protect travelers, barges, and small communities, the fort system was later expanded when Congress authorized construction of railroads across the plains. After the Civil War, the forts became centers for new communities, as some travelers and a few enlisted men's families decided to stay.

"The West" as a concept thus came to typify the last frontier. In the process, it became not only a place but also a mythological part of the American psyche, celebrated in song and story. It became a cultural identifier uniquely dissimilar to the urbanity of New York City, the industrial dynamism of Chicago, or the agricultural fiefdoms of pre–Civil War Georgia. The West became a unique, if generalized, part of the continent's

All decked out in "wooly" chaps and a fancy vest,
this theatrically dressed cowboy is ready to face the camera,
if not the dirty and dangerous work on the frontier.

history and culture. It became the place from which, according to observers such as historian Frederick Jackson Turner, we sprang as a nation: an open, wonder-filled place that continues to permeate modern life and stimulate our national self-concept. In popular stories, it was settled by characters of strength, durability, and purpose who were almost all white. Of course, reality was much different. Instead of passively accepting such myths, we should search out the facts of our past. Truth and historical perspective are essential to helping us assess the past—to learn who we are, where we came from, and perhaps where we are going.

James Beckworth

Not many black men rose to the level of "legendary" in the American West, but Jim Beckworth was an exception. In fact, Beckworth's life was so extraordinary, he is now considered an American hero.

A freed slave and the son of a white transplanted St. Louis blacksmith, Beckworth spent his early years listening to the tall tales of French Canadian explorers who came down the Missouri and Mississippi rivers to trade. In 1824 he asked his father what he should do with his life, and was told to follow his heart.[1] Later that year he signed on with William H. Ashley's expedition out of St. Louis as a wrangler and manservant. It was only a short association; within a year, he was an independent trapper buying furs from Pawnee Indian traders.

Beckworth ventured westward, sharing the vast areas of the Great Plains and the Rockies with Jim Bridger, Kit Carson, Jedediah Smith, and other mountain men. He was not the only African American to take up the solitary trade as a mountain man: Edward Rose and Dred Scott—whose slavery indenture was later upheld by the U.S. Supreme Court—also sought their fortunes in the high mountains.

Beckworth's achievements in the wilds of the West culminated in 1834 when he became a chief of the Crow Indians. It was a position he held for seven years—an almost unheard-of honor for a non-Indian. He married "Sue," a Santee woman, discovered the pass in northern California and Nevada that bears his name, and pioneered the Oregon Trail through Crow country. In later years, he opened a bar and other businesses in a small village on Cherry Creek, which would become Denver, Colorado.

Beckworth recorded his western exploits in *The Life and Adventures of James T. Beckwourth: Mountaineer, Scout, and Pioneer* (1856), blending factual stories with the garrulous and often outrageous tales that mountain men perfected into an art form.

Frontispiece from *The Autobiography of James Beckworth*. Note the anglicized features when compared to the photograph in the preface.

2

Early Imagery

The Society of Friends [Quakers] were the first, I believe, in
America, who publicly denounced slavery as incompatible
with the Christian religion; and slave holders as unqualified
to become worthy members of their truly religious society.

— George Washington Ogden, "Letters from the West"

PHOTOGRAPHERS in the American and Canadian West faced assignments that were extremely demanding, lonely, and treacherous. Cameras and developing equipment were not only large and clumsy but also fragile and expensive to maintain. Portrait photographers in out-of-the-way settlements made a living on the small charges they assessed for informal, or "nonstudio," images, which were eventually recognized as an inexpensive substitute for the costly oil portrait. Consequently, a traveling photographer earned not only an income but also the title of "artist."

It is difficult to imagine how those artists, who drove wagons loaded with cameras, film, glass plates, caustic chemicals, and repair supplies, managed on a day-to-day basis. Yet they seemingly covered the American West, Canada, and Alaska with alacrity and efficiency. Their work exists in thousands of images that have survived for more than a century, and one can assess much more about the everyday life of the past from informal photographs than from portrait photographs.

Typically, an itinerant photographer—there were but few women who practiced this trade—entered a town with little advance notice. If there was a newspaper, a photographer might take out a small advertisement to announce his arrival. More likely, however, he relied on simple word of mouth or performed some services gratis to gain attention. He likely visited the local saloon, looking for potential customers in the barroom who might want the ubiquitous "family portrait." By offering the

This image, drawn from life by an artist for *Harper's Weekly* in the 1860s,
depicts a group of Shakers dancing with what is probably a runaway slave
(*figure on extreme right*) joining in. The Shakers were noted for assisting
runaways who were traveling north on the Underground Railroad.

bar patrons a chance to have their pictures taken—ordinarily outdoors,
in front of a saloon or hotel where the sun shone and the camera setup
was quick and easy—the photographer recorded not only scenes of everyday happenings but also inadvertent evidence of African American
men, women, and children as part of the cultural life. Such images show
life on the streets of western settlements as a far greater amalgam of differing social and ethnic groups than popular culture has generally allowed.

Beginning in the late 1700s, publications employed itinerant sketch
artists, painters, and lithographers to add visual variety to solid pages
of newsprint. Artists such as Frederic Remington earned substantial incomes and acclaim for their drawings. Popular nineteenth-century publications put lithographs on the front page of nearly every issue. Later, they
dedicated even more images to pictures of contemporary events.

Images played an important role in telling the story of the Civil War.
Newspapers and periodicals sent correspondents, sketch artists, and even
some photographers to the battlefields to cover the engagements. Although innovations in printing did not make photojournalism possible
until the late nineteenth century, engravings based on Civil War battle-
field photographs captured the public's imagination. Mathew Brady, for
one, depicted the drama and horror of the war, and his famous photographs, as reinterpreted in the papers by engravers, were as powerful in
reporting events as any written description.

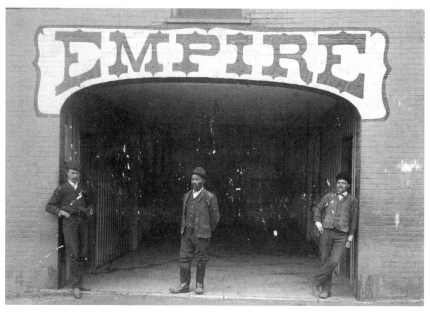

Life in western settlements was more ethnically diverse
than in many of these same towns today.

"Massacre of Chinese at Rock Springs, Wyoming—Drawn by T. de Thulstrup
from photographs by Lieutenant C. A. Booth, Seventh United States Infantry"
(*Harper's Weekly,* September 26, 1885). The scene depicts white miners revolting against
the hiring of Chinese to work in the coal mines. The result was several hundred
Asian dead, most killed by bombs placed in the mine shafts while they worked.

"Come and Join Us, Brothers," one of the most well-known recruiting posters of the Civil War, successfully encouraged young black men to join the Union forces.

(Courtesy of the National Archives, Washington, D.C.)

Black soldiers stand guard outside a southern business taken in a military siege.

(Mathew Brady photograph, courtesy of the National Archives, Washington, D.C.)

A rare image of Americus Haynes, a "buffalo soldier"
from Vancouver, Washington.

THE PHOTOGRAPHS

Locating nineteenth-century photographs of African Americans in the West, Canada, and Alaska is a difficult task. Professionals made the earliest-known photographs including tintypes, daguerreotypes, ambrotypes, glass-plate negatives and glass-slide positives, cartes de visite, cabinet photographs, and others. Few bore any identifying information.

Provenance remains another troubling issue. Although some photographs have information about the subjects and locales written on the back, most do not. Information about the subjects, their occupations, and social status can often be deduced from clues such as background details, type of photograph, and location, but until further research unearths more relevant material, the description of many photographs remains incomplete.

Young Bat and Mrs. Slaughter relaxing inside a shed, circa 1885.
Individuals of many racial heritages and cultures existed side by side
in a time not generally remembered for interracial socializing.

(Courtesy of the John Slaughter State Park, Arizona.)

＊ ❈ ＊

Several issues surround the use of the word *race*. Beyond skin color, a person's racial heritage can assume social, political, geographic, religious, and cultural importance. A person's search for his or her roots begins with whatever racial and cultural heritage is relevant. The search for pictorial images of black westerners likewise involves recognizing which ones were relevant and which were not. Although it may seem obvious that one image appears to be a black person and another is not, it is not that simple.

The Antwerp Saloon, Portland, Oregon, circa 1888.
The Antwerp was primarily a meeting place for members of the Belgian
community but obviously was not limited to their patronage.

(Courtesy of the Oregon Historical Society, Portland.)

A quick review of census records from the nineteenth century reveals that the census takers were not always explicit or precise in their written commentaries. Their use of such terms as *Negro, African, mulatto, half-breed, octoroon,* and others is, invariably, confusing, inexact, and prejudicial. Quite often these records reflect a census taker's highly personal impressions of race or ethnicity. Other times, the individuals themselves seem to have provided the information.

Since the original intention was to include a wide variety of pictorial images, this book does not base its selections on the terms used by census takers. Images of individuals who identified themselves as black were accepted at face value and are included. A statement by a contemporary who seemed to have no ulterior motive in describing another as "Negro" also validated the image for inclusion. For those images lacking provenance, selection was difficult, so they must stand alone on their merits. Thus, this volume includes images of individuals who are identified as being black, who appear to be so, or who were attested to by family and friends as being black. ▪

3

Black Westerners in
White Mythology

IN THE NINETEENTH CENTURY, newspaper reporters, sketch artists, and photographers described westerners and their lives. These reporters often blended fact and fiction to create a population of Caucasian sheriffs, city builders, ministers, and entrepreneurs with whom their primarily eastern readers could identify, thereby giving birth to the myth that the West was inhabited primarily by whites. The growing popularity of dime novels and periodicals, and, much later, radio, motion pictures, and television, added to the illusion that the West was white.

The media seldom covered the roles played by African American men and women as explorers, expedition guides, managers, and ranch hands. Although the Lewis and Clark expedition in the early nineteenth century and the Ferdinand Hayden mapping expedition into the Rocky Mountains in the 1870s employed African American men in important positions, these facts were not generally known until well into the twentieth century.

Readers of newspapers, magazines, and other print media acquired an enhanced, or "popular," image of the West and its inhabitants with the addition of graphic art to the various media. But this false depiction contributed to widespread misperceptions of the social roles of blacks, American Indians, Asians, and Latinos in western history.

THE FIRST IMAGES

The first pictorial representations of African Americans published for predominantly white audiences were of slavery. The most popular antebellum periodicals—*Harper's Weekly, Canadian Illustrated, Puck,* and *Leslie's Illustrated Weekly,* for example—published lithographic engravings (the first "photographs") of African American slaves. The words and pictures most often validated the prevailing attitudes of whites toward blacks.

Kansas became the focus of many blacks who moved west.
This style of studio portrait, which was not uncommon despite
being expensive, helped change stereotypes of African Americans'
outward appearance in the white media of the day.

Women washing clothes for the military during the Civil War. Such images strengthened stereotypic impressions of African Americans. (*Harper's Weekly,* January 16, 1864.)

These woodcuts typify how the media depicted slave auctions.

Highly popular throughout the country, stereoview cards from the late 1800s usually portrayed black individuals as thieves, children in need of supervision, menial laborers, wastrels, or in other demeaning characterizations. These images were often the only ones many whites saw of African Americans.

An Arbuckle "Ariosa Brand" coffee card, circa 1890. These pocket-size cards were used by traveling salesmen as a "humorous" gimmick. The coffee prices were listed on the reverse side of the card.

NO GROUNDS FOR COMPLAINT.

FARMER—"Hi, there! Can't you see that sign—'No fishing on these grounds?'"

COLORED FISHERMAN—"Co'se I kin see de sign. I's cullid, boss, but I ain't so ignerant as ter fish on no groun's. I'm fishin' in de crick!"

From *Texas Siftings*, by permission.

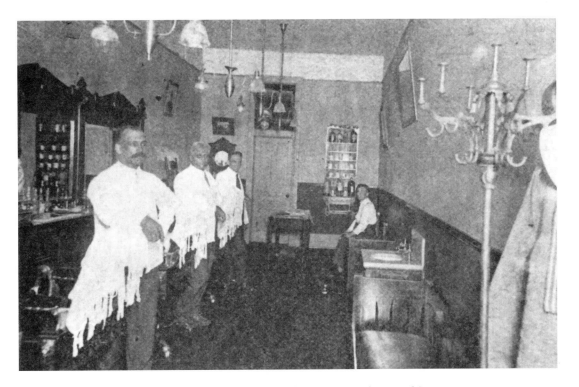

Barbering was essentially a "black" occupation in the United States
prior to 1900, as this image from Ann Arbor, Michigan, illustrates.
Only after the turn of the century did it become "white."

After the Civil War, when freed men and women began to look for
work, they found Irish, English, German, and Scandinavian immigrants
already holding the better-paying jobs. Thus, photographs of the time
usually showed black workers performing only menial tasks.

WESTERN ROLES

Itinerant photographers of the late 1800s enjoyed much the same stature
as the lithographers and sketch artists who had preceded them. In the
West, photographers found a ready audience for their skills, employing
glass plates and sensitized sheets of copper to capture images of people
in formal and everyday poses. Although most of the subjects were white,
many were people of color.

The U.S. military provided many opportunities for African Americans. The so-called buffalo soldiers were often seen protecting wagon
trains venturing west.

Flatboats were used on the shallow rivers of the West for ferrying materials and travelers.

(Courtesy of the Montana State Historical Society, Helena)

Photography was among the many technological developments of the nineteenth century. A few black entrepreneurs entered this business, as did W. L. Goodridge of Saginaw, Michigan, circa 1900. He is probably the man shown leaning in the doorway.

Most likely photographed in the studio shown
above, this cabinet card is typical of its time.

The westward movement also brought murder, injustice, and violence with it. In particular, competition for work led to conflicts based on racial prejudice. Any individual, regardless of ethnic background, was "brought to justice" if believed guilty of a perceived violation of the law. Although relatively rare in the West, lynchings of lawbreakers, white and black, took place from time to time.

The picture was not entirely bleak, however. Entrepreneurs established hotels, schools, newspapers, and other enterprises. Barney Ford, a former slave, became a Colorado innkeeper. In Trinidad, Colorado, in the 1890s, Nancy Phillips, a nurse and midwife, tended to patients of all ethnic persuasions.

A saloon in North Dakota, circa 1890. This photograph illustrates the
inclusion of African Americans in the everyday activities of western life.

(Courtesy of the North Dakota State Historical Society, Bismarck.)

Wagon train near Saratoga, Wyoming, circa 1890. Unlike the well-provisioned
groups of whites, African Americans often trekked westward with minimal
supplies and few guides, following in the wagon tracks of others.

(Courtesy of Dick Perue Historical Photos, Saratoga, Wyoming.)

Drawing from Associated Press Release.

XI. One More Lynching In Laramie

There was the time after the turn of the century when the townsmen used the rope again.

Confined in the county jail in August, 1904, was "a human degenerate Joe Martin, negro" using the name of Joe Smith. He had just served three years in the Wyoming penitentiary (now relocated at Rawlins) for a bestial crime.

Judge Carpenter had sentenced him to six months in the local jail for sending obscene letters through the mail. On this particular day he was caught in a lynching web of his own brutal instincts.

The wife of Sheriff Alfred Cook had engaged a sixteen-year-old girl, Della Krause to assist her in the courthouse kitchen. Della was peeling potatoes when she heard a loud scuffling noise behind her. Turning she saw Joe Martin coming at her. The prisoner had managed to spring the lock of his cell by prying it with the steel coil from the springs of his cot. He had in the same manner been able to open a cupboard of general use in which was kept shaving items. He had grabbed a razor and now came slashing at Miss Krause.

The sheriff's wife hearing the screams rushed to the scene just as the girl with her throat gashed open slipped to the floor. Mrs. Cook grabbed the negro's arms and was able by sheer strength to pinion him, all the while yelling for help.

Sheriff Cook and a deputy came running and the captive was beaten into submission and cast back into his cell, but not before he had with suicidal intentions haggled his own throat and was wallowing in his own blood.

Dr. Stevens was summoned and pronounced Della would live, but would be disfigured for life. The Boomerang put out a special edition of the fiendish attack, and all afternoon men huddled together on a street

A lynching in Green River, Wyoming, 1895.

(Courtesy of the Wyoming State Museum and Archive, Cheyenne.)

Unfortunately, lynchings were a part of the western experience. This 1904 event, in Laramie, Wyoming, resulted from a vicious attack (and subsequent jailbreak) on a white woman by Joe Martin, a black prisoner. He was hanged by a local mob.

(Courtesy of the American Heritage Center, University of Wyoming, Laramie.)

Barney Ford, a hotelier, entrepreneur, gold miner, and civic leader in Wyoming and Colorado, who also served as a member of the statehood committees for both states.

(Courtesy of the Wyoming State Museum and Archive, Cheyenne.)

"Aunt" Nancy Phillips, a nurse and midwife in remote Wyoming gold-strike towns, became a beloved resident of Rock Springs and Green River near the turn of the twentieth century.

(Courtesy of the Sweetwater County Library, Green River, Wyoming.)

Job opportunities kept pace with the growing businesses in western towns. In Texas, for example, these men found work as draymen.

(Courtesy of the Collins Street Bakery, Corsicana, Texas.)

Johnell Jenkins of Elysian, Texas, displays the blending of traditional Mexican dress in this image of a Texas cowboy at work.

Ned Huddleston, better known as Isom Dart, a bandit
and rancher, lived and worked in the Colorado, Utah, and
Wyoming area in the late 1880s. Some legends claim he was shot
and killed by the notorious Butch Cassidy near Brown's Hole
in northwestern Colorado. Yet another story places his demise
near Wolcott, Wyoming, after a failed bank robbery. Students
of photographic history should note that this image, though
seemingly authentic, contains the wrong firearms for the period
and was most likely a staged portrait for the tourist market.

(Courtesy of the Savery Museum, Savery, Wyoming.)

There were also black outlaws. Former slave Ned Huddleston was a
rancher, broncobuster, and gambler before he changed his name to Isom
Dart and became a cattle rustler. Stories of the deeds of Isom Dart and
other African American outlaws merged with those of their white con-
temporaries, becoming part of western legend and lore.

❧ 4 ❧

Black Photographers
in the West

AFRICAN AMERICANS also worked as photographers in the West, although in very small numbers. Some of these photographers had moved
previously established businesses from the East; others learned the trade
by working with field photographers employed by newspapers, calendar
printers, and stereoview-card manufacturers. Assistants often appeared in
the photos so that human scale could be added to the otherwise immense
vistas being recorded.[1]

This chapter will focus on some of these black men and women who
moved along with the general exodus of Americans into what was then
thought of as "the West," that is, prior to 1840 or so, anything west of Pennsylvania. In most cases they left scant traces of their passages; however, a
few stand out as successful artists and businessmen.

LUCIUS HARPER

We know little about Lucius Harper, an obscure photographer from
Galveston, Texas. Only two examples of his work survive, and they are
scarred and timeworn. The images of his two sons Amos and Lucius Jr.
(photographed ca. 1910) display an interesting and effective use of light
and display his technical proficiency as a commercial portraitist. Further-
more, his images underscore the fact that photography had entered the
mainstream of American life.

Cabinet card of Lucius
Harper Jr., circa 1900.

Cabinet card of Amos
Harper, circa 1900.

James Presley Ball was one of the premier photographers of the American West, as is evident in this photograph of an unknown woman.

"The Narrows of Williams Canyon, Manitou, Colorado, 1901," a stereoview card by the H. C. White Company. Stereoview photography ordinarily used large-format negatives (usually eighty-by-ten-inch glass plates) as the master. Before being published and sold, these images were cropped to smaller sizes to suit the demand. The huge negatives make large enlargements possible, which often reveal details not readily seen. The man shown was a photographer's assistant.

Little is known about this image
other than that it was produced
by John Green in Denver.

A nonstudio image by John Green.

JOHN GREEN (CA. 1880–CA. 1930)

Denver's John Green was another black photographer.[2] Very few of his
images have survived. Like that of Lucius Harper, Green's work is not the
product of a true "studio photographer" but rather that of a talented amateur who charged little for his services and produced images of a casual
nature.

Self-portrait of Richard Harry Shepherd, shown on
the reverse of one of his cabinet cards, circa 1889.

RICHARD HARRY SHEPHERD (1854–UNKNOWN)

Richard Harry Shepherd moved from Virginia to St. Paul, Minnesota, and
is another example of a black photographer who brought skills learned
elsewhere to the wilds of the West. In less than a decade, he simultaneously owned or co-owned three separate photography parlors, one of
them in cooperation with James Presley Ball, a mixed-race photographer
from Cincinnati. Shepherd allegedly boasted that he made nearly twenty
thousand dollars a year, a tremendous salary in 1899. Shepherd falls in the
middle ranks of black photographers of his time, locally extolled but na-
tionally unknown. Though hundreds of his images exist today, he disappeared into history when he moved—apparently to Chicago—in 1905, as
documentation of his work after that is difficult to find.

This cabinet card of an unidentified black man is an unusual example of the quality of Shepherd's work in St. Paul, circa 1889, when he co-owned a studio whose major clients were white.

Elaborate gold-leaf stamping further identifies Shepherd's work. His emblem, an *H* with a superscript *S,* looks more than a little like a dollar sign. He proudly reproduced gold medals won at the 1891 state fair.

The only known photographic image from life of James Presley Ball (*second from right*) and his brother Thomas (*second from left*). This stereoscopic view was taken at Cornell's Studio, in New York, probably when Ball was visiting in the late 1860s.

JAMES PRESLEY BALL (CA. 1825–1904)

Students of African American photography consider James Presley Ball an icon. Born in Virginia, most likely as a freeman, he took up photography early in life and met the black daguerreotypist John Baily in 1845. Within a year he opened a "daguerrean" studio in Cincinnati, the first of a series of relocations westward. He soon closed his studio and began traveling throughout the East, specializing in daguerreotypes and portraits.

In 1849 he joined his brother Thomas—and, later, his brother-in-law, Alexander Thomas—in operating studios in Cincinnati. His son, James P. Ball Jr., trained early in the business and joined his father while he also read for the law, which he practiced later throughout the country and Hawaii.[3]

Ball published an antislavery monograph in 1855 to accompany a six-hundred-foot-long panorama illustrating black history that was displayed

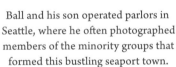

Ball and his son operated parlors in
Seattle, where he often photographed
members of the minority groups that
formed this bustling seaport town.

This scalloped-edged cabinet
card contains almost as much
advertising as portrait, circa 1890.

in his gallery.[4] The booklet, *Ball's Splendid Mammoth Pictorial View of the
United States Comprising Views of the African Slave Trade,* was available at
the showing of the painting. His photographs of Frederick Douglass were
widely distributed across the country.[5]

Ball returned to Cincinnati for a short time, where he was associated with the black artist Robert Scott Duncanson, whose Hudson River
School landscapes rank among the best of America's artistic legacy. Duncanson operated a photo studio in Cincinnati as an adjunct to his painting
and apparently worked with Ball on projects that resulted in both photographic images and paintings of the same subjects.

An abolitionist before the Civil War, Ball lectured widely on the evils
of bondage and traveled wherever he thought his presence might help advance the cause, even serving as a delegate to a civil rights convention.[6]
On at least one occasion, he and his son traveled to aid a black school in
Mississippi, where they were denounced as "carpetbaggers" and "scamps"
for apparently absconding with undue cash.[7]

This cabinet card from Ball's first Seattle studio shows another example of vignetting (the "scroll" is associated with memorial cards), with yet another change in address and card style.

In Seattle, these children struck a relaxed pose. Many of Ball's extant images are of children.

In late 1879 Ball moved to Minneapolis, where he met and worked with Richard Harry Shepherd for a short time. Newspapers of the era reported that "Prof. Ball" was widely received as a photographer and had become active in political circles.

In 1887 Ball left for a lengthy trip overseas. He eventually returned to the States and opened a shop in Helena, Montana, J. P. Ball and Son at the Sign of the Red Ball.

As the images illustrate, Ball did a substantial business photographing women. A cursory view of existing Ball photographs shows a predominance of women and children as subjects.

Ball's repertoire of "everyday" people includes relatively few images of African Americans. Few blacks lived in Montana, and even fewer could afford photographs.

Apparently in poor health, Ball moved to Seattle around 1900, where he opened the Globe Studio, in conjunction with his lawyer son and

An ethereal quality
seems to suffuse this
carte de visite of Derri
Anna Simpson in a
richly brocaded dress.

A carte de visite of a "mulatto"
or mixed-heritage woman
photographed by Ball in
Cincinnati, circa 1860.

J. P. Ball & Son,   Helena, Montana,
OPPOSITE POSTOFFICE.

⇒◉•SIGN OF THE RED BALL•◉⇐

Photographed in a parlor at yet a different address for Ball's studio, this
young woman displays a silk taffeta dress and a stylized cavalry saber
at her throat. The Ninth and Tenth Cavalries were stationed in the
area throughout most of Ball's tenure. Could this have been a wife or a
daughter of one of those men? Ball's photographs of black subjects are
the most difficult to find today, since few could afford his services.

daughter-in-law, Laura, who had come to the Puget Sound area in the early 1890s. Together they operated two parlors before moving yet again, to Honolulu, possibly for the older man's health. Although directories list Laura Ball as a photographer on King Street and elsewhere, no images bearing her name or that of Ball and Son of Honolulu have been discovered.

In 1904 James Presley Ball died in Honolulu. The cause of death was listed as "ascites," a condition commonly brought about by cirrhosis or deterioration of a major organ. Daguerreotypists commonly suffered debilitating diseases because of the powerful and deadly chemicals used in the process.

Among the more interesting information about the Ball family is the fact that his granddaughter Alice Augusta Ball (1892–1916) was the first woman of any ethnicity to earn a master's degree from the University of Hawaii. Almost forgotten by history, she discovered a treatment for leprosy in an extract of chaulmoogra oil.[8]

WILLIAM HINES FURBUSH (CA. 1839–1902)

If any figure of the past fulfills the promise of high drama, legendary derring-do, political ambition, and—oddly enough—photography, it was William Hines Furbush.[9] Born into slavery in Kentucky, he was owned by a newspaper editor and later by the mixed-race John James Audubon, the great naturalist. When Audubon died, Furbush gained his freedom and began practicing photography in Delaware, Ohio. During the Civil War, he traveled widely throughout the South and Midwest.

In February 1865, Furbush enlisted in the Forty-second Colored Infantry at Columbus, Ohio, and traveled with his regiment to Kentucky, where it was attacked by Confederate forces. After the attack, Furbush distinguished himself by tending to wounded fellow soldiers.

In 1866, disillusioned and worn down by the war, Furbush emigrated to Liberia as part of the American Colonization Society's effort to return blacks to Africa. By 1870, however, he was back in the States, working as a photographer in Arkansas and making a sizable income.

He ran as a Republican for the state legislature and was elected by dint of his articulate, educated manner, as newspapers of the day reported. He was a strong antisegregationist and engaged in legislative—and physical—battles when denied services because of his race. He and others even sued for their rights in at least one court case—and won. In 1872 he was named the first sheriff (of any color) of Lee County, Arkansas. He carried a firearm for personal protection and led a faction of one hundred men in the so-called

The only known image of William Hines Furbush.

(Courtesy of the Marion/Lee County, Missouri, Museum.)

Brooks-Baxter (liberal Republican versus conservative Republican) War. He later alienated fellow blacks by switching to the Democratic Party.

Subsequently, his life included political intrigue, an assassination attempt in which he was stabbed in the back, allegations of a murder or two, being fired as sheriff for failing to follow a court order and for several random shootings of citizenry, and a move to Denver and Bonanza, Colorado (where he was arrested for murder and later exonerated).

An extremely rare image taken by
William Hines Furbush in Ohio

A. S. Thomas,

166 W. Fifth St.,
CINCINNATI, O.

The A. S. Thomas daguerrean studio
replaced Ball and Thomas after 1869.

After returning to Little Rock, he practiced law; attended the 1888 Republican National Convention in Chicago (he was thrown out for being a "Democratic plant"); edited the *National Democrat,* an African American newspaper; and killed yet another man in an argument. Furbush eventually fell on hard times and, in 1902, died in a veterans' home in Nashville.

Ball's Great Daguerrean Gallery of the West. James Presley Ball's Cincinnati studio
as depicted in *Gleason's Pictorial Drawing-Room Companion* (April 1, 1854:208).

Alexander S. Thomas (ca. 1820–ca. 1900)

In late 1852 Alexander Thomas arrived in Cincinnati from New Orleans; he met and married Elizabeth Ball, the sister of J. P. Ball Sr. His famous brother-in-law hired him as a receptionist, and within two years Thomas was working in the daguerreotypist's studio and laboratory as an "operatist." Next, he opened an office with the senior Ball, giving the business two studios. "Ball & Thomas" became a premium brand and stamp for the photography trade in Cincinnati. Together, they produced thousands of cabinet cards, daguerreotypes, cartes de visite, tintypes, and, much later, silver albumen prints. According to at least one source, the city's "best families" patronized the firm, and the two men often had more business than they could handle. Unfortunately, in 1860 a tornado destroyed their studio, causing the duo financial ruin. Friends and colleagues came to their aid, however, and a new parlor rose out of the destruction—"the finest photographic gallery" west of the Alleghenies.[10] They prospered as a team until the older man left for Minneapolis in 1869. Afterward, Alexander Thomas operated his own studio at the original location.

✸ 5 ✸

Warriors and Soldiers

Buffalo Soldiers

DURING THE CIVIL WAR, more than 186,000 African American men served in the Union army under the banner of the United States Colored Troops. Despite low pay and inadequate equipment, the First South Carolina Volunteers, the Fifty-fourth Massachusetts Infantry, and other black Union regiments fought valiantly. However, after the war, black soldiers found that, unlike their white counterparts, they were not eligible for pensions or other benefits. Most found themselves discharged from the service and left to fend for themselves. Some who stayed in the army were reassigned in the West. Until the end of the nineteenth century, these "buffalo soldiers," as they came to be known, served in segregated units under the command of white officers.[1] Based in the plains and the Southwest, these enlisted men fought the Sioux, Apaches, Comanches, Kiowas, Kickapoos, and other Indians; protected the southern border with Mexico; and guarded westward-bound wagon trains.

The U.S. military fort system was established to protect migration routes in support of western expansion. The buffalo soldiers of the Ninth and Tenth Cavalries regularly rotated through almost all of the western forts, with especially long stays at Fort Robinson, Nebraska; Fort Sill, Oklahoma; Fort Huachuca, Arizona; Fort Jefferson Davis, Texas; and Fort D. A. Russell, Wyoming.[2]

Immediately following the Civil War, the War Department formed four black units to serve primarily in the Southwest.[3] (Originally, the Thirty-eighth through the Forty-first Infantries were designated "colored." Within a matter of months, however, they were regrouped into the Twenty-fourth and Twenty-fifth Infantries and the Ninth and Tenth Cavalries.) Army commanders concluded that black soldiers should be limited to assignments below the fortieth parallel. Army brass held to the

Edwin Byron Atwood, sergeant major of the Forty-
first Ohio Infantry, fought in the battles of Murfeesboro,
Tennessee; Chickamauga, Georgia; and Mission Ridge,
Tennessee. Here he poses for his mustering-out photo.

myth that men of African descent would never tolerate the colder northern climate.

Although it is unclear where the term *buffalo soldier* originated,
black troops liked the sobriquet, and the Ninth and Tenth U.S. Cavalries
proudly called themselves buffalo soldiers until the 1930s, when the last

Troopers of the Ninth Cavalry in
California. This is from a stereoview
card and is one of many depicting
black soldiers in the late 1800s
and early 1900s in the West.

Bird Baker,
a buffalo soldier.

Many African American troopers—like these of the Tenth Cavalry from Fort
Huachuca, Arizona, depicted by Frederic Remington (*second from right,* his three
hundred–pound girth reduced by artistic license)—stayed on in the West, forming
a corps of trained horsemen who joined the expanding cattle kingdom.

(Courtesy of the American Heritage Center, University of Wyoming, Laramie)

The Tenth Cavalry football team at Fort Robinson, Nebraska,
home of buffalo soldiers for nearly forty years.

(Courtesy of the Nebraska State Historical Society, Lincoln.)

The Twenty-fourth Infantry at Fort Reno, Oklahoma Territory, circa 1890. There are even fewer known photographs of the two black infantries, the Twenty-fourth and Twenty-fifth, than there are of black cavalry units. Both infantries were formed after the Civil War.

(Courtesy of the Fort Sill Museum, Oklahoma.)

of the mounted troops disbanded to become armored divisions.[4] Later, black infantry soldiers proudly adopted the name.

In the late nineteenth and early twentieth centuries, the American Southwest was the scene of singular military experiments with firearms, clothing, transportation, and maneuvers. In Arizona, for example, the U.S. Cavalry studied the use of camels for desert warfare. The army even experimented with bicycles, and black troops were among the first to ride the new contraptions. Units of the Tenth Cavalry from Fort Huachuca in Arizona and the Twenty-fifth Infantry from Fort Missoula in Montana tested bicycles as a means of military transportation. For a year several groups started from the northern Rockies in Montana and toured southward, crossing Wyoming, Colorado, and New Mexico. The experiment eventually failed, but it left some of the most intriguing photographs of African American troops ever seen.

A rare close-up of a black soldier wearing an authentic buffalo-hide coat.

(Courtesy of the Coe Library, Reference Section, University of Wyoming, Laramie.)

"The Charge Up San Juan Hill," Chicago Lithographic Company.

Soldiers of the Ninth and Tenth Cavalries are shown working on a building in
Fort Washakie, Wyoming, which was the central town on the Shoshone Indian
Reservation. Many of the buildings constructed by the soldiers still stand.

(Courtesy of the Wyoming State Museum and Archive, Cheyenne.)

The James A. Moss group of the Twenty-fifth Infantry Bicycle Corps from Fort Missoula,
Montana, in Yellowstone National Park, October 1896 (Photographer: F. Jay Haynes).

(Courtesy of the Haynes Foundation Collection, Montana Historical Society, Helena.)

Original tintype of a "black Mexican,"
apparently taken in Mexico.

NEGRO-SEMINOLE SCOUTS OF
THE TWENTY-FOURTH INFANTRY

Runaway slaves often found their way west with the help of Florida Seminole Indians, some going as far as Coahuila, in northern Mexico.[5] In the
early 1870s, federal officials persuaded them to return to the States, and the
black Seminoles recrossed the border into Texas. Some of these repatri-
ates enlisted as scouts with the Twenty-fourth Infantry at Fort Duncan.[6]

In 1914 the assistant secretary of war requested that these scouts and
their families be added to the rosters of enrolled Seminoles and be subsequently granted deeded lands. The Interior Department denied the
request, however, and the black Seminoles ended their military careers
largely unknown and unrecognized. ▣

Original cabinet photograph (circa 1895) of Negro-Seminole
Indian scouts, by J. M. Stotsenberg.

(Courtesy of the Ben E. Pingenot Collection, Brackettville, Texas.)

These buffalo soldiers appear to be part of a musical unit, ready to entertain
as needed. Since they are both heavily armed and mounted on a large military
cart, it might be assumed they were a permanent fixture in the services.

6

Cowhands and
Ranch Hands

TODAY, THE MEDIA portray African American cowboys in motion pictures, television programs, and magazine articles, but they were largely overlooked in the nineteenth century, even in the stories and songs of the day. (See Chapter 15, "The Entertainers.") Historians estimate that between three and nine thousand black cowboys worked on just one of the western cattle trails, the Goodnight-Loving "Long Trail" from West Texas to Montana Territory, during the halcyon days of the "cattle kingdom," roughly 1860 to 1910.[1]

African American cowhands worked a variety of jobs—not just menial ones, which is a common misconception. Many of these men hailed from southern farms and plantations and were especially skilled in training and vetting horses. When herding cattle, black cowhands often rode point, which was a position of honor since the rider would be ahead of the dust clouds stirred up by the cattle.

Cooks were important to life on the range, as they fed hungry and demanding cowboys daily. Cowboying was a tough and boring grind for the young men riding herd, and with towns and settlements miles distant from the trail, cowboys of all colors and ethnicities could become unruly and difficult to control. Consequently, cooks prepared a variety of appetizing and satisfying meals as well as desserts ranging from fresh fruit pies to candy and sweet drinks.

Cooks demonstrated their combined skills in food storage and preparation, knowledge of sources of food on the trail, and a general ability to control their rambunctious young comrades. Many western ranches had talented black cooks who worked there—often for decades.

African American cowboys also showed off their musical talents. Cooks, especially, entertained by playing fiddles, harmonicas, and guitars in camp. Many noteworthy cow-country musicians were black—contrary

This handsome cowboy embodies the mythology of the black man
in the West, even as it may record a somewhat idealized image.

to the images of white singing cowboys in western films of the 1930s and
1940s. The popularized legendary singing cowboy was often a former slave
who relied on his singing talents to calm nervous cattle.[2]

Rolf Logan, who rode the range on his trusty horse Roundup, was a
northern California cowboy of the 1800s. ▨

These black cowboys worked on the A. E. Gillespie Ranch, in southern Wyoming.

(Courtesy of W. Gordon Gillespie, Laramie, Wyoming.)

Black jockeys racing horses in Cheyenne, Wyoming, near the turn of the century.
Black cowboys were commonly employed as jockeys during this time.

(Courtesy of the Wyoming State Museum and Archive, Cheyenne.)

"Ick" the trail cook, by J. R. Thomas. "Out Our Way" was a popular comic
strip from the 1920s to the 1940s. In it, the artist portrayed scenes from his life
as a cowhand, replete with characters drawn from his personal experience.
"Ick" was amazingly free of most stereotypes in popular cartooning of
the time. He spoke in dialect, and so did the other cowhands.

Jess Stahl, bucking-horse champion and purported creator of
"hoolihanding," a particularly athletic means of wrestling a steer
to the ground, using acrobatic flips and turns, circa 1900.

African American cowhands at work in Wyoming and Colorado.

(Courtesy of the LaFrantz Collection, American Heritage Center, University of Wyoming, Laramie.)

Black cooks were common on ranches in nearly every western state.

(Courtesy of the Wyoming State Museum and Archives, Cheyenne.)

This photograph of a man playing the guitar captures the
essence of a tradition with a long history.

Rolf Logan on his horse, Roundup, circa 1890.
Well-known throughout northern and central California,
Logan was a pioneering cowboy and homesteader.

(Courtesy of the California State Library, Sacramento.)

Rolf Logan branding cattle.

(Courtesy of the California State Library, Sacramento.)

7

Women of the West

BLACK WOMEN faced as much or more racism and prejudice in the West as black men. They also suffered from the societal restrictions placed on women in general in the nineteenth century.

SOME POSITIVE EXPERIENCES

Born a slave in Tennessee in 1832, Mary Fields moved to Toledo, Ohio, after the Civil War. There, Fields worked for an Ursuline nun named Mother Amadeus, a childhood friend. When Mother Amadeus went to Montana, Fields soon followed, arriving in 1885 in what would become the small town of Cascade. Fields preferred the company of men to the Catholic sisters, however, and she eventually struck out on her own. She quickly earned a reputation for her rough-and-ready demeanor, becoming one of the most interesting, individualistic, and determined women of the era.

Standing six feet tall and weighing some two hundred pounds, Mary Fields brooked little challenge in her jobs as laundress, barkeeper, and cigar-smoking Wells Fargo shotgun rider in Montana and northern Wyoming. She possessed the personality traits necessary for survival in those days and places: high spirits, independence, and toughness. Nevertheless, despite her rough disposition, Fields befriended most of the townspeople in Cascade. The town's children loved her, and the adults trusted her for her honesty and her devotion to local causes. One biographer noted that, when Fields died in 1914, "there was no shortage of pallbearers for the tough but kind black woman who had befriended generations of local children."[1]

Clara Brown was born a slave in Spotsylvania County, Virginia, in 1800. Years later, she earned her freedom, and in 1857 she found her way to Kansas Territory. Two years later Brown moved to Central City, Colorado, where she opened a laundry, using her profits to invest in local gold mines. She soon founded an African Methodist Episcopal church, which met in her home, and opened a Sunday school, the first in Colorado. Noted for her kindness and gentle nature, "Aunt" Clara soon earned a reputation as "the angel of the Rockies."

A frugal woman who kept her own counsel, she acquired inexpensive land around Central City as well as around the cattle and Indian town of Denver, consisting at the time of little more than canvas-covered buildings and tepees around Cherry Creek. She frequently grubstaked miners who had no other means of support while they looked for gold in the mountains west of Denver. Those who struck pay dirt repaid her handsomely for her kindness and generosity. She used any profits to continue her philanthropy among the needy and to increase her landholdings.

When a flood destroyed the records of those landholdings, she could not prove ownership and subsequently lost title to much of her property. In addition, dishonest business rivals found her vulnerable to their unscrupulous deals, especially after her property records were destroyed. Eventually, she lost everything, but no one whom she had helped over the years let her suffer from hunger or lack of friendship. Whether rich or poor, landholder or not, "Aunt" Clara Brown emerged as one of the true legends of the nineteenth-century Rocky Mountains.

❦ ❦ ❦

Mary Ellen Pleasant, better known as "Mammy Pleas," was an early pioneering woman. She resented the appellation, considering it an overly familiar form of address. Many others, however, called the mercurial businesswoman from San Francisco an "angel of the West" for her work with troubled and abused women, men, and children.

Born a slave in Virginia about 1817, young Mary Ellen somehow found her way to freedom in Massachusetts ten years later. The mixed-race girl began passing for white. By the late 1840s she was actively involved in the antislavery movement. By 1852 she had made her way to San Francisco. A complex and emotional woman, Pleasant spent large sums of money to aid fugitive slaves and freedmen. She fed them, found them jobs, and financially backed them in numerous small businesses. She also protected abused women, building and supporting women's havens in California. Following the Civil War, Pleasant changed her racial designation in the city's directory from white to black, and she began campaigning for black civil rights. She died in January 1904.

Some Adverse Experiences

Black women in the West also ran afoul of the law. Eliza Stewart was sent in 1899 to the territorial prison at Laramie, Wyoming, for shooting at her paramour—and missing. A large woman, recorded in prison documents as "weighing over 200 pounds," Eliza served time in the equivalent of a federal penitentiary for an assault for which few, if any, white women were ever charged. She served twenty-one months before being released.

Caroline Winfield Hayes served two sentences in the penitentiary, the second for twenty-one months for an unspecified crime. A mere two weeks after her release, she stole two fifty-cent blankets from a local store and was arrested again. This time, authorities incarcerated her in the local jail and then sent her home to Cheyenne.

Other women were convicted of nonviolent crimes such as stealing bread or small articles of clothing. Most were released after a few months for such reasons as ill health, good behavior, or because they had become pregnant.[2]

Prostitution

Prostitution was a powerful force in the development of many western communities, and a source of personal wealth and political influence.[3] Black brothels existed alongside white ones in many settlements. In Laramie, for example, black women operated and staffed the "1000 Grand" at the corner of Grand Avenue and First Street.

One legend claims that a black woman named Emily D. West, an indentured servant, was the inspiration for the 1858 minstrel version of "The Yellow Rose of Texas":

> *There's a yellow rose in Texas that I am going to see,*
> *No other darkey knows her, no darkey only me;*
> *She cried so when I left her, it like to broke my heart,*
> *And if I ever find her we never more will part.*

She's the sweetest rose of color this darkey ever knew,
Her eyes are bright as diamonds, they sparkle like the dew,
You may talk about your Dearest May, and sing of Rosa Lee,
But the yellow rose of Texas beats the belles of Tennessee.

THE AULTMAN PHOTOGRAPHS

Three white men, brothers Oliver, Otis, and Everett Aultman, owned one of the longest-lasting photographic studios in the American West, in Trinidad, Colorado, near the foot of Raton Pass, nudging the New Mexico–Colorado border.[4] The area served as a haven for lawbreakers in the West and a home to miners from Greece and England. Railroads, stagecoaches, teams of oxen and wagons, and cowboys passed through this funnel-shaped area, heading north toward more populated areas.

The Aultmans opened their photographic studio in 1889 and began one of the most remarkable ethnographic collections in the country. Their photographs preserved the images of the people who lived in this small, ethnically rich town in a hollow of the Rockies. The photos recorded the lives and varied occupations of whites, African Americans, Chinese, Japanese, Mexicans, American Indians, and others. These images are carefully posed studio photographs, in contrast to the inexpensive, casual snapshots associated with itinerant photographers.

The Aultmans became known for their willingness to accept subsidies for their work. Often, someone other than the subject of the photograph paid for the session. Their photographs are therefore ordinarily identified not by the names of their subjects but by the names of the local individuals who subsidized preservation of this multicultural town's history.

The nineteenth-century African American women whom the Aultmans captured on film were generally unnamed, but their images here represent a selected gallery of the varied roles played by black women in the early days of the West.

Stereotypes of African American women were perpetuated by images like this one in an 1800s stereoview card. The figure is not a woman but a white man in blackface, wearing women's clothes. The stereoscope was a popular item of entertainment in the parlors of whites who were enamored of this three-dimensional viewing device.

Accurate images of black women's appearance and roles
were unknown to most whites of the times and apparently
ignored when they were available. This attractive "Gibson
girl" is a well-dressed woman who could afford to have
her picture taken in a Los Angeles studio, circa 1890.

Teaching was one of the professions open to African American women,
especially in remote parts of the West. Here, an unnamed woman stands
on the plains of northern Wyoming, circa 1890.

(Courtesy of the J. Guthrie Nicholson Jr. Collection, American
Heritage Center, University of Wyoming, Laramie.)

"Aunt" Clara Brown, a Colorado pioneer in the
gold-mining towns of the Rockies.

(Courtesy of the Colorado State Historical Society, Denver.)

Mary Fields on the streets of Miles City, Montana, circa 1895.
Of the five known images of Fields, only this photo shows her with a shotgun.

(Courtesy of the Ursuline Centre, Great Falls, Montana.)

Mary Fields became a successful businesswoman in times when both gender and
color limited opportunities. This photo shows Fields around 1895, in one of her
characteristic hats, behind her favorite horse, probably in Miles City, Montana.

(Courtesy of the Ursuline Centre, Great Falls, Montana.)

Mary Ellen Pleasant.

(Courtesy of the San Francisco Public Library, San Francisco, California.)

A typical occupation for an African American woman in the West was that of midwife. Sybil Harber achieved prominence for her skill as a midwife in her hometown of Lakeview, Oregon, in the late 1800s.

(Courtesy of the Oregon Historical Society, Portland.)

This unusual image purports to show a frontier black midwife, ready for her duties.

Women in western prisons were few in
number. An unknown female prisoner
is shown here in "formal" pose.

Eliza Stewart was known as "Big Jack" to her friends and comrades.

(Courtesy of the Wyoming State Museum and Archive, Cheyenne.)

Caroline Hayes (also Winfield), a native of Ohio, served time in the Wyoming territorial prison in Laramie.

(Courtesy of the Wyoming State Museum and Archive, Cheyenne.)

Images of black prostitutes are rarely found and clearly bear no
identifying marks as to their profession. However, Victorian
rules of dress and demeanor dictated that women who exposed
their limbs and affected devil-may-care attitudes were exhibiting
characteristics frowned upon by more genteel society.

Provocatively dressed, this woman is identified in
the records of the Colorado Historical Society as
a prostitute from the Trinidad, Colorado, area.

(Courtesy of the O. E. Aultman Collection, Colorado Historical Society, Denver)

This woman, dressed in a typical nurse's uniform
at the turn of the twentieth century, apparently
worked in the Trinidad, Colorado, area.

O. E. Aultman opened his
photographic studio in 1889.

8

The Adventurers

York

IN HIS JOURNAL Meriwether Lewis recorded the following about William Clark's slave, York, who accompanied the men on their journey of discovery to the Northwest:

> One of the men had spread the report of our having with us a man perfectly black, whose hair was short and curled....
>
> We assured him it was true, and sent for York. Le Borgne was very much surprised at his appearance, examined him closely, and spit on his finger and rubbed the skin in order to wash off the paint; nor was it until the negro uncovered his head and showed his short hair, that Le Borgne could be persuaded that he was not a painted white man.
>
> The object which appeared to astonish the Indians most was Captain Clark's servant York, a remarkably stout, strong negro. They had never seen a being of that color, and therefore flocked round him to examine the extraordinary monster. By way of amusement, he told them that he had once been a wild animal, and caught and tamed by his master; and to convince them showed them feats of strength which, added to his looks, made him more terrible than we wished him to be.[1]

Records indicate that York was especially skilled with horses, and, although not a translator for the expedition, it seems that he developed an "ear" for American Indian languages. York apparently had very dark skin ("black as a bear," wrote trader Pierre Antoine Tabeau) and was a curiosity to the Indians Lewis and Clark encountered.[2]

A Currier and Ives print showing York, a slave of William Clark,
unloading boats on the Platte River, circa 1885.

Mountain men of color
traveled the mountains
and plains of the West, as
did this unnamed man.

Legends about York abound. Rumor had it that he was a juggler and gymnast (probably true), a master of several Indian tongues (unlikely), larger than normal in size for his time (probably true), handsome (possibly), and popular with Indian women; he reportedly left several mixed-race offspring in his wake.

ISAIAH DORMAN:
GUIDE, TRANSLATOR, MILITARY HERO

Some twenty-nine films tell the story of George Armstrong Custer's monumental defeat at the hands of superior Indian forces on the Little Bighorn River in Montana. None of these movies suggests that a black man participated in that infamous event. But in fact Isaiah Dorman, a black man, served as an interpreter for Major Marcus A. Reno, whose troops engaged in a fight with Indians some three miles south of the main battle.

Serving as guides from the earliest days of discovery, black men like Dorman accompanied U.S. geological mapping surveys, army expeditions, and other western excursions. Nearly as common as black cowboys, these guides, outfitters, hunters, provisioners, cooks, instructors, and foremen are noted in accounts of the time, including many photographs.

Isaiah Dorman, however, does not appear in any authenticated photographs, which is surprising since he served with Custer on various private and military expeditions for a number of years. What little is known about Dorman derives from a few short texts about "Custer's black white man." The passages refer to Dorman's skill with Plains Indian languages and his work as a translator and guide on sundry government expeditions. He was so valued for his skills that he got three times the pay of most soldiers.[3]

Thomas O'Sullivan, a white contract photographer for the government, documented several mapping and military expeditions in the 1800s throughout the Southwest, Montana Territory, and the Yellowstone area. One of his photographs depicts a young black man and what may be Apache guides. The man could be Dorman, though no one knows for sure. He wears the traditional garb of guides of the time and has—according to "Dorman apocrypha"—two of Dorman's three recorded although rather generally described physical attributes: a very wide nose and an extremely large chest. Yet another individual who might be Dorman sits behind this man in the photograph. Or it might be Dorman who appears in the background of another photograph taken on Custer's 1874 Yellowstone expedition.

Isaiah Dorman's gravestone marks the site of his death at the Battle of the Little Big Horn. Although virtually all other death sites at the national monument were given markers prior to the 1940s, Dorman's was put in place in the 1950s. His was the last stone to be erected.

An unidentified black guide and Indians, circa 1873, in the Yellowstone area, photographed by Thomas O'Sullivan.

(Courtesy of the U.S. Geological Survey Photographic Archives, Denver.)

Members of Custer's Yellowstone expedition. Note the man standing behind the group by a tent who could be, but most likely is not, Isaiah Dorman. Nonetheless, his presence shows the importance of civilian guides to western military campaigns.

(Courtesy of the South Dakota State Historical Society, Pierre.)

Digitally enhanced close-up of the figure by a tent in this photograph of Custer's Yellowstone expedition members. (Later analysis of this image indicates that it may be that of any of several guides assigned to Custer.)

If an image of Isaiah Dorman is to be found anywhere, it is probably in this photograph
of Custer's Seventh Cavalry taken within a year of the infamous battle at the Little Big
Horn River in southern Montana. Dorman may well be one of the men on white horses.

(Courtesy of the National Archives, Washington, D.C.)

This Mathew Brady photograph shows Custer (*right*) and Lieutenant James B. Washington, a Confederate prisoner, alongside an unidentified black child.

(Courtesy of the Library of Congress, Washington, D.C.)

The Custers and Lucy (last name unrecorded), their cook. The photograph was taken at Fort Lincoln, Montana Territory.

(Courtesy of the North Dakota State Historical Society, Bismarck.)

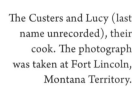

Throughout his career George Custer fostered numerous relationships with African Americans as military aides and civilian camp employees. At home and on the trail, Custer and his wife, Elizabeth, employed black cooks, dog handlers, and handymen. Elizabeth Custer described one cook, Lucy, in her diaries. Another black cook, Mary Kercherval (discussed later), worked for the Custers at the time of the famous battle; she and Elizabeth stayed behind at Fort Lincoln.

OTHER GUIDES AND HUNTERS

In the late 1800s the U.S. Congress subsidized several discovery expeditions to the West. Ferdinand Vandeveer Hayden and John Wesley Powell captained equally important scientific ventures. They focused mainly on geologic formations, with a strong emphasis on the vast region's potential for economic development.

Hayden led several mapping expeditions of Yellowstone and the Gallatin Forest in what is now southern Montana. These expeditions recorded the geology, flora, and fauna of an area that would later become Montana, Wyoming, Idaho, and parts of Colorado. One Hayden expedition photograph includes artist Thomas Moran, an army officer, and an unidentified black man—the group's provisioner. Typically, a provisioner supplied and maintained tents and firearms, tended horses and livestock, and provided fresh meat.

Even less is known about the members of the Tenth Cavalry who worked on a contingent assigned to map the area that would later become Yellowstone National Park. The black troopers safeguarded the surveyors and scientists on the expedition. The photographs of those guardian "rangers" appear here in print for the first time.

Members of the Clarence King survey party, mapping the fortieth
parallel, circa 1868–1870. This group shows the multiracial
makeup of many government expeditions.

(Courtesy of the U.S. Geological Survey Photographic Archives, Denver.)

Members of Ferdinand Hayden's expedition of 1869–1870, probably in southern
Wyoming Territory or northern Colorado. General Cook is in the robe, and
Thomas Moran is seated near the tent. The black man is the group's provisioner.

(Courtesy of the American Heritage Center, University of Wyoming, Laramie.)

On Hayden's expedition of 1871, Joe Clark, seen in this close-up, was
a hunter assigned to the crew. He is mentioned several times in the
logbooks of the expedition kept by its surgeon, Dr. Albert C. Peale.

(Photo by W. H. Jackson. Courtesy of the U.S. Geological
Survey Photographic Archives, Denver.)

The Tenth Cavalry from Fort Huachuca, Arizona, was assigned to
protect the first mapping expeditions of the Yellowstone area, circa 1880.

(Courtesy of the Teton County Historical Society, Jackson, Wyoming.)

❖ 9 ❖

Across the Country's Interior

All Colored People
THAT WANT TO
GO TO KANSAS,
On September 5th, 1877,
Can do so for $5.00

Announcements such as this appeared as placards, posters, and newspaper advertisements in midwestern and eastern states to encourage black migration to Kansas.

ON APRIL 30, 1803, representatives of the United States signed the Louisiana Purchase, which acquired from France all or portions of what would become fifteen states. This purchase made vast westward expansion across the continent possible. Following the Civil War, freed black slaves joined whites who were moving into these territories.

ROBERT BAILEY

One pioneering family, the Baileys, settled on the far western edge of South Dakota, near Edgemont.[1] Robert Bailey served with the Tenth Cavalry in Wyoming and Nebraska as well as in the Spanish-American War. After returning from the Philippines, he served out the remainder of his enlistment with other black troops at Fort D. A. Russell in Cheyenne, Wyoming. In 1909, Robert and Ella Mae, his wife, settled in South Dakota. In order to amass more acreage, they homesteaded separate but adjoining claims and began to "prove up on them," in compliance with the law. One

13641—Cowboy, Bronco Corral and Camps, Banks of the Yellowstone, Montana, U. S. A.

Black cowboys in Montana (*above*) and California (*right*). These cabinet cards, a popular photographic format in the nineteenth century, illustrate the contributions of African Americans to an expanding America.

(Lower image courtesy of the California State Library, Sacramento.)

In 1909, Mary Fristo eloped with Henry Blakey, leaving Salisbury, Missouri, and moving to Yankton, South Dakota. She is shown here with her son Arthur Raymond.

(Courtesy of Ted Blakey, Yankton, South Dakota.)

Brothers James and Zacharias (Bud) Blakey selling vegetables in Yankton, South Dakota, after the turn of the twentieth century.

(Courtesy of Ted Blakey, Yankton, South Dakota.)

Ted Blakey with Ronald Reagan, 1980, when Blakey was a representative
to the Republican National Convention. Blakey was a lifelong Republican and
self-made businessman. Ted died in 2004, in his beloved Yankton.

(Courtesy Ted Blakey, Yankton, South Dakota.)

Allen Chapel, African Methodist Episcopal Church, Yankton,
South Dakota. This was the Blakey family's congregation; it remains
today as a rare example of black churches of the time.

Robert Bailey, circa 1890, in his Sunday best,
shortly after he had homesteaded in western Nebraska.

(Courtesy of William Bailey III, Edgemont, South Dakota.)

William "Bill" Bailey III, circa 1917.

Roland and Beatrice Kercherval, circa 1910, in Edgemont, South Dakota.
(Courtesy of Beatrice Kercherval, Edgemont, South Dakota.)

of their children, William B. "Bill" Bailey III, enjoyed a long and color-
ful life, which included serving as a buffalo soldier in the last years of the
horse cavalry and owning a casino in Reno, Nevada.[2]

THE KERCHERVAL FAMILY

In 1873 young Mary Kercherval and her son, Charles, traveled to the
Dakotas with the Seventh Cavalry. Mary was George Custer's personal
cook and began working for the Custers at Fort Dodge, Kansas.[3] Later,
the two would accompany the Seventh to Fort Rice, Dakota Territory,
where Custer's forces protected engineers of the Northern Pacific Railroad. Charles cared for Custer's horses and dogs (the lieutenant colonel
traveled with racing hounds and peacocks).

When Custer's troops later left Fort Abraham Lincoln for the Black
Hills, Mary and Charles stayed behind with Mrs. Custer. After the Battle of Little Big Horn, Mary remained in Bismarck, where she purchased
a 120-acre homestead near Spearfish. There is no verified photograph
of Mary Kercherval, although a few "possibles" can be found in South

Bass Reeves, lawman.

(Courtesy of the Coe Library, Reference Department, University of Wyoming, Laramie.)

Dakota. Charles and his wife, Elizabeth, raised nine children on the old homestead.

Born a slave in Oklahoma and descended from French Creole and Apache ancestors, Beatrice Cotton migrated west with her family soon after emancipation. Beatrice married Roland Kercherval, a son of Charles and Elizabeth Kercherval. The couple lived in a succession of towns in eastern Wyoming and western South Dakota, where they farmed and raised cattle, turkeys, grain, and hay. Beatrice also worked occasionally in Sheridan, Wyoming, and in Buffalo, South Dakota.

BASS REEVES

The term *hero* sits well on the broad shoulders of Bass Reeves. Standing six feet, two inches tall, and weighing two hundred pounds, he proudly wore a deputy marshal's badge, pinned to his breast pocket by U.S. Marshal James F. Fagan at Fort Smith, Arkansas in 1875.

Born a slave near Paris, Texas, in 1838, Reeves developed a notable proficiency as a fighter and wrestler. In his thirties he got into an argument with his master, knocked him out, and fled across the Red River

Deputy U.S. marshals who served the District Court of the Western District of Arkansas, with jurisdiction in Indian Territory. Sworn in at the same time as Bass Reeves were (*left to right*) Amos Maytubby, Zeke Miller, Neely Factor, and Bob L. Fortune.

(Courtesy of the Denver Public Library, Western History Collection, Denver.)

Hester and Charles Meehan,
the first homesteaders in
Cherry County, Nebraska.

(Courtesy of the Great Plains Black
Museum, Omaha, Nebraska.)

Mary Hall Reese, who walked
from Kansas to Nebraska
City, Nebraska, after being
freed from bondage. She was
a founder of the AME church
in Nebraska City in the 1870s.

(Courtesy of the Great Plains
Museum, Omaha, Nebraska.)

toward freedom. There, in Indian Territory, he formed close relationships with Seminole and Creek Indians.

Later, Reeves caught the eye of Marshal Fagan, who also deputized other marshals of color such as Zeke Miller, Bud Ledbetter, and Grant Johnson (half Indian, half black, called the "mulatto from Eufaula") to deal with an increasing number of crimes committed by newly freed black men and unruly white land speculators who had flocked illegally to Indian Territory in search of cheap land.

Reeves employed a unique style as a lawman: he used disguises and pretense to catch criminals.[4] Known for his guile and inventiveness in tracking criminals (he reportedly handcuffed a group of seven outlaws while they slept), Reeves earned fame for his extraordinary successes as a lawman. He was also known for his ambidextrous skill with pistols, excellent horsemanship, and convincing use of aliases. In his career, Reeves arrested more than three thousand lawbreakers, collecting rewards on many of them.[5]

WAGON TRAINS

The sides of the trail were lined with negroes, headed for Topeka and Emporia, Kansas to get a free farm and a span of mules from the State Government. Over my pack there was a large buffalo robe, and on my saddle hung a fine silver-mounted Winchester rifle. These attracted the attention of those green cotton-field negroes, who wore me out asking questions about them. Some of these negroes were afoot, while others drove donkeys and oxen.

— Charles Siringo, *Riata and Spurs,*
describing what he witnessed in 1879

White settlers composed most wagon trains heading west. This may have been less a matter of racism (although it probably was an issue) than of economics. To purchase a heavy-duty wagon (the trusty Conestoga, for example), clothing for the journey and the destination, food for three to seven months' travel, oxen, horses, and mules and to pay a share of the guides' expenses could amount to the modern equivalent of thirty thousand dollars or more, clearly beyond the means of most freed blacks.

Earliest known photograph of African Americans in the Nebraska Territory, 1865.

(Photograph by C. W. Walker. Courtesy of the Nebraska State Historical Society, Lincoln.)

Understandably, however, their newly gained freedom fed their wish to journey westward to new lands. Banding together without highly experienced guides and with minimal equipment, black wagon trains followed the wheel ruts of the white pioneers who preceded them.

The Chadron Photographs

In 1906, Ray W. Graves set up his photo parlor in Chadron, Nebraska. The images he recorded there included local citizens, Indians, scenic views of the plains and bluffs of northern Nebraska, and a rare black doll—obviously, the pride of some child. More than eleven hundred glass plates, tintypes, and negatives have survived and remain in the collection.

Like most small towns in the West, Chadron was home to African Americans. Some of them, as is apparent in the Graves photographs, achieved a relatively high level of income and acceptance in the community. The photographs of Chadron's black citizens (all of them unidentified) are few in number, which likely reflect their limited representation in the community.

The poor physical condition of the photographs reproduced here illustrates the ephemeral nature of photography. Poor storage facilities, water damage, and other factors nearly wiped out evidence of the African American experience, but now the photo archives at Chadron State University's library and other such institutions provide haven for these photographs and other valuable artifacts of the black experience in the American West.[6]

Just as African Americans emigrated to the prairies and plains to work as farmers, sheepherders, and cattlemen, in the arid Southwest black families joined other hardy newcomers—notably former soldiers and scouts—who braved the rigors of dry deserts and high mountains. Many of their descendants remain there today.

In the 1800s black adventurers, explorers, and cowboys traveled throughout the

Photo of an unidentified black man from Ray W. Graves's Chadron, Nebraska, photo parlor. After 1906.

Photo of schoolchildren in Chadron, Nebraska. Note the black child in the center. Ray W. Graves photo, after 1906.

Photo of a rare black doll.
Chadron, Nebraska. Ray W.
Graves's studio, after 1906.

Mrs. Charles Soper, circa 1870,
is photographed in her role
of nursemaid to a white child,
one of the most common
employment opportunities
for African American
women in the West.

(Courtesy of the Sharlott Hall
Museum, Prescott, Arizona.)

Old Mammy's Christmas Lesson

"Nanny" images such as that at left often showed the idealized and the more pedestrian, while the frontier image below was far more accurate.

A Texas nanny and her employer.

Rocky Mountain West. James Beckworth trapped in the Cache Valley of northern Utah and southern Idaho. Isom Dart rode with Butch Cassidy and the Sundance Kid in the area called "Brown's Hole" (now Browns Park) encompassing parts of Colorado, Wyoming, and Utah. Jacob Dodson accompanied John Frémont's expeditions in the 1840s. Black cowboys such as Albert "Speck" Williams, Nat Love, and one of several men called Deadwood Dick (who spent his last years as a Pullman porter based in Salt Lake City) lived and worked in the region.

When the Mormons began leaving Nauvoo, Illinois, in 1846 to find and settle in what they called "Zion," or "the Promised Land," a few black men and women joined the entourage. According to legend (and a few facts), former slave Green Flake drove the wagon in which Brigham Young lay ailing during the trip through the pass above the valley of the Great Salt Lake. Whether the story is true or not, former slaves Flake, Hark Lay, and Oscar Crosby did ride with that emigrant wagon train making its historic way into the Salt Lake Valley. Flake was likely not a member of the Church

A black soldier and three Navajo scouts who worked out of Fort Verde, Arizona, and probably Forts Wingate and Whipple. This style of studio portrait was popular; it was usually sent home to the family as a remembrance.

(Courtesy of the Fort Verde State Park, Arizona.)

Inside the guardhouse at San Carlos, Arizona. The man on the right, a trooper in the Ninth Cavalry, is wearing his field dress, which was regulation since the heavy woolen military uniform was impractical in Arizona's climate.

(Courtesy of the Sharlott Hall Museum, Prescott, Arizona.)

A carte de visite of Nancy Simpson from Prescott, Arizona, on the back of which is written, "This is one of the girl's sayings, 'Well, I must go home pretty soon. In fact, sooner than that. Will be back right away.' Miss Nancy Simpson now Mrs. Richardson February 23, 1868. Nancy Simpson who worked 3½ years for us in Junction, Arizona."
(Courtesy of the Sharlott Hall Museum, Prescott, Arizona.)

of Jesus Christ of Latter-day Saints at that time, but rather a friend and entrepreneur who helped Mormon emigrants from Nauvoo reach their new homeland.

Prominent blacks listed in Mormon history included Franklin Perkins, born in 1813; George Stevens; and George Bankhead, the son of a white slave master. Bankhead converted to the Mormon Church and moved with his sons to Draper, Utah, in 1852. Elijah Abel, a black man who attained a high position in the church in Nauvoo as a member of the Quorum of the Seventy, moved his family to "Zion" and helped build the Mormon temple in Salt Lake City.

Of the black towns established in the American West, Dearfield, some forty miles northeast of Denver, Colorado, was one of the most unusual. Founded by black businessman Oliver T. Jackson in 1909, Dearfield was so named because Jackson claimed the land was dear to all who lived there.

The town grew quickly, fueled by the need for truck-farm products in the Denver area. Black families built houses, a restaurant, gasoline station, store, dance hall, and saloon. The town's dance band became well known throughout the region. Crops grew abundantly. Travelers of all ethnicities

"Renegade Negro" photograph
by Wittick Studios, circa 1883.
Note the fake background of
this studio portrait, a common
practice of early photographers,
who often supplied the subject
with inaccurate dress and firearms.
The object was to promote
sales to eastern customers.

(Courtesy of the Arizona
Historical Society, Phoenix.)

Black soldier with water wagon.

(Courtesy of the Fort Verde State Park, Arizona.)

Mrs. Emma Wright (Knight?), circa 1880, wearing a quasi-military dress she undoubtedly fashioned herself. It was common for women's formal dress to incorporate chevrons, as both a stylistic element and as an acknowledgment of a military connection.

stopped in the town on their way to other places. Although the town no longer exists, foundations from some of its original buildings can still be found west of Greeley, Colorado.

Black cowboys such as Thornton "Thornt" Biggs were not uncommon in Wyoming, but few homesteaded or bought land. Some did settle in Wyoming, however, including ranchers Alonzo and Esther Stepp (LaBarge), James Edwards (Manville), and George Jordan (northern Albany County). Matthew Campfield (Casper) was a successful politician and businessman. Others, such as midwife and nurse Nancy Phillips (Green River), became prominent in their communities.

Barney Ford was an entrepreneur who owned hotels in Cheyenne and Denver, and he was a member of the statehood commission in 1889. Nolle Smith, born in 1889 and raised on a ranch north of Cheyenne, became a notable member of Hawaii's legislature in 1929. Few other black men or women held elective offices in Wyoming until 1988, when voters elected Elizabeth Byrd of Cheyenne to the legislature.

Near the Montana border, William Fields, a black man, tired of the racism and living conditions in Sheridan, Wyoming. He found 320 acres of vacant "coal land" available for platting and in November 1915 began building what he thought would be a complete town. The original plat map from Cat Creek lists some one hundred or more names and the small plots assigned to each,

African American soldiers and white officers preparing to
ride into the Arizona high country, circa 1890.

(Courtesy of the Fort Verde State Park, Arizona.)

Summer camp at Fern Springs, August 21, 1887. Summer camps in the high
country around Fort Verde were a welcome relief from the heat in lower
elevations. Black nursemaids tending their small charges were a common sight.

(Courtesy of the National Archives, Washington, D.C.)

Schoolchildren in Prescott, Arizona, circa 1895.

"Estevan," as depicted in a nineteenth-century allegorical
painting of Spanish troops and an American Indian.

(Courtesy of the Tuskegee University Archives, Alabama.)

Elderly John Slaughter and family, circa 1900, with the man called "Old Bat" near rear center.

(Courtesy of the John Slaughter State Park, Arizona.)

Riders from the Slaughter ranch, which had a contract with
the U.S. government to maintain the Mexico-U.S. border in that area.

(Courtesy of the John Slaughter State Park, Arizona.)

Henry Ossian Flipper, circa 1876, the first African American graduate of West Point. He was later drummed out of the cavalry on trumped-up charges. He migrated to Slaughter's ranch, where he worked as an engineer. Revetments that he constructed can still be seen on the property.

(Courtesy of John Slaughter State Park, Arizona.)

"Old Bat," who lived most of his life with John Slaughter both on the ranch and when Slaughter was sheriff of Tombstone, Arizona.

(Courtesy of the John Slaughter State Park, Arizona.).

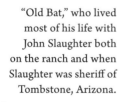

119

Samuel D. and
Amanda L. Chambers,
early Mormons in Utah.

(Courtesy of the Church of Jesus
Christ of Latter-day Saints Historical
Department, Salt Lake City.)

Green Flake, an early black
pioneer in Utah Territory. This
grainy newspaper halftone
is the only known image of Flake.

(Courtesy of the Church of Jesus Christ of Latter-
day Saints Historical Department, Salt Lake City.)

Captioned in the archives as "Taken at Utah Pioneer Jubilee, Salt Lake City, July 24, 1894." The group "Utah Pioneers of 1847" includes the African Americans (*far left*) seen more closely in the inset.

(Courtesy of the Church of Jesus Christ of Latter-day Saints Historical Department, Salt Lake City.)

Hard-rock miners in some forgotten quarry in the West.

Ben Palmer, the first black rancher in Nevada Territory, circa 1855.
With him is Mary Hawkins, a local resident.

(Courtesy of the University of Nevada, Reno.)

Porter was among the limited job categories readily open
to black men in the early years of railroading.

including Carl Settlers, a former buffalo soldier from Cheyenne; Jess
Baker, stepson to John Lewis; Bob Springfield, a black Crow Indian;
Avelina Harris; Calley Stone; John Ivy; and James Askew.

Most never developed their land, and few built structures. It was probably more of a dream than a reality, but the idea of an all-black community
in Wyoming attracted many investors. By the late 1920s nearly everyone
had moved away from the little community or sold their property to one
of the large cattle ranches in the area. Marie Lewis remained in Sheridan,
the sole surviving settler.

Stereoview card of the Ninth Cavalry, stationed at Fort Garland, Colorado, circa 1890.

(Courtesy of Ed Bathke, Manitou Springs, Colorado.)

R. J. von Dickersohm, a former Zulu
chieftain and emigrant to Colorado.

Residents of Dearfield, Colorado, circa 1935. Founder Oliver T. Jackson is at far right.
(Courtesy of Geraldine Stepp-Evans, Denver.)

This Real Photo Post Card image is most likely that of Fred
Riley on the streets of Saratoga, Wyoming, circa 1915.

George Jordan, circa 1915. Jordan was a pioneer rancher and amateur engineer whose innovative ranch and irrigation system can still be seen in remote northern Albany County, Wyoming.

(Courtesy of the Wyoming State Museum and Archives, Cheyenne, Wyoming.)

Matthew Campfield, circa 1900. Campfield, a Civil War veteran who lost a leg in battle, was a pioneering merchant and politician of Casper, Wyoming.

(Courtesy of Casper College, Casper, Wyoming.)

Branding cattle on the John A. G. Lewis Ranch, Cat Creek,
Wyoming. Lewis was one of a small group of men and women who
founded a small community east of Sheridan, Wyoming.

Cat Creek, Wyoming, as photographed by the author in 1995.

Esther Yates Stepp and Alonzo Theodore Stepp,
circa 1920, LaBarge, Wyoming.

(Courtesy of Geraldine Stepp-Evans, Denver.)

The Stepp Family Ranch

The Fontenelle Creek area of western Wyoming was the setting for that rarest of occurrences in the American West: a cattle ranch owned and operated by a black family.[7] African Americans commonly worked on ranches, but seldom owned them. In Wyoming vast expanses of open grazing land, little water, scant forage, and sparse population impeded ranching. Not to be deterred, a black man named Alonzo "Lon" Stepp tried his hand at ranching in western Wyoming. Born in Berea, Kentucky, in 1872 to former slaves Archie and Ann Moore Stepp, Lon grew up in a society that—although segregated—allowed him to gain an education and experience denied to many persons of his race. He enrolled in the racially integrated Berea College in 1893 and took classes in Christianity, mathematics, history, American government, composition, rhetoric, Latin, and Greek.[8] In his first year at Berea, he met and fell in love with Esther Yates.

This image, taken by Geraldine Stepp in the late 1940s, shows a part of the Stepp Ranch.
(Courtesy of Geraldine Stepp-Evans, Denver.)

During the summer of 1893, Lon was invited to work on the Rathbun Ranch on Fontenelle Creek, some ninety miles north of Rock Springs, Wyoming. Rathbun had gotten word that Lon had exceptional talents and wanted him to learn the cowboying trade.

After working a year on the ranch, Lon returned to Berea, where he married Esther and stayed for about four years. They welcomed three children during that period. The lure of the West, however, had taken hold of the young man, and Lon decided to return to Wyoming, where he became top hand at the Rathbun Ranch. He mastered his job so well, in fact, that Rathbun helped him to acquire land and livestock of his own. Lon saw that good land existed along the Green River bottom, which stretched like a grassy sliver through the brown, dry landscape, and he thought that would be a good place to start his own cattle business.

It took Lon and Esther three years to build a cabin and start a business, time in which Lon rode fifteen miles every day from their small cabin to work on the Rathbun Ranch. He also worked as a barber in nearby Opal, Wyoming, to supplement the family's income. His father and mother, Archie and Ann, and brother Willard soon joined them in the West.

With Rathbun's aid, the Stepps "proved up"—built a cabin, dug a well, and made other improvements—on a plot of ground along the Green

Archie Stepp, shown in this cabinet
card, was reticent about his years as
a slave and talked little about them.

(Courtesy of Geraldine Stepp-Evans, Denver.)

This cabinet card shows the Stepp family, circa 1920,
posed in front of the "Old Place," the homestead cabin.

(Courtesy of Geraldine Stepp-Evans, Denver.)

River. Archie, Ann, and Esther also established their own homesteads that later became part of the growing ranch, which the family ever after called the "Old Place."

For a while, Lon worked part of the time for Rathbun and tended his own land and a small herd of sheep. The young man considered the fifteen-mile ride to work every day worth the effort. Eventually, when Rathbun purchased more sheep and needed to graze them around neighboring Montpelier, Idaho, Lon would go on trail for months at a time, leaving his small acreage in the care of Esther and the two oldest sons, John and Bill.

By 1918, seven children lived with their parents on the ranch: Helen, John, Bill, Nell, Ruth, Grace, and Horace (known in the family as Dutch). Archie had died two years earlier at the age of eighty-five, and Ann died shortly afterward. By the early 1920s, Lon secured a loan from an area rancher, John Chrisman, and the First National Bank of Kemmerer (Wyoming) to purchase an additional 750 acres of deeded land from Dan Robertson and 1,500 acres grazing rights from the Bureau of Land Management, bringing the ranch's size up to what would be considered a medium to large operation in that part of Wyoming, even by today's standards. His ranch specialized in raising and selling yearlings for the commercial beef market. The family even built a new ranch house, situated upstream from the Old Place, on the lush edges of the Green River, with soil that literally burst with growth when Lon and his family planted trees, bushes, and a small garden. Geraldine Stepp Evans, widow of Lon's son Bill, later wrote that "the land surrounding the ranch house encompassed over an acre which he fenced and planted with sixty cottonwood trees; they grew magnificently and gave the landscape an aura of beauty."[9]

The 1920s, '30s, and '40s proved to be good years for the Stepps. The ranch prospered as the boys assumed more and more control of operations. A third generation began to take root, as the sons married and raised their children as Wyoming ranchers. John, Bill, and Dutch married and stayed on the ranch itself or nearby, whereas the women, Helen, Nell, Ruth, and Grace, moved away. All, however, kept the ranch central to their lives and returned for family gatherings and ranching festivities whenever possible.

They were a popular family, part and parcel of the area's social and religious scene. Lon even sponsored religious services in his house, which were attended by families from nearby ranches. He also founded the first permanent Methodist church (not AME) in nearby LaBarge. They counted the Herschlers—whose son, Ed, would be both the Stepps' attorney and,

The "New Place," as photographed by Geraldine Stepp-Evans, circa 1949.
Note that the Wyoming Stock Growers Association membership sign
reads "John Stepp," Lon and Esther's eldest son. In 1976 the president of
the association informed the author that the Stepps were the only African
Americans to hold membership in the organization up to that year.

later, governor of Wyoming—as close friends. Lon, undoubtedly one of
the most educated men in Lincoln County, also served as deputy assessor
for many years and as postmaster of the Fontenelle Post Office, which was
located at the ranch. The children all attended one-room ranch schools.

Lon's ranch also served as a center for entertainment. Each of the children learned a musical instrument: Dutch played the organ and piano;
Bill, drums; John, guitar; and Grace, piano. Together with Lon, who
played the mandolin, the group provided the music for weekend dances
and picnics all across the area. Later, in the 1950s, John, Bill, Dutch, and
Ralph Armstrong (a neighbor who played saxophone) toured western
Wyoming as far north as Jackson to play at various events.

Racial problems seldom intruded onto the Stepp Ranch, or into the
family. Although of a different racial makeup than most other residents
of Wyoming, the Stepps resembled all the others when it came to ranching, and they became well known throughout western Wyoming for their
strong sense of family and community, and for being the only black members of the Wyoming Stock Growers Association.[10] Even today, family

Branding time on the Stepp Ranch.

(Courtesy of Geraldine Stepp-Evans, Denver.)

The Stepp Ranch today. Compare this image taken by the author with the
earlier image of the ranch house taken from the same viewpoint.

Alonzo and Esther Stepp, circa 1940.
(Courtesy of Geraldine Stepp-Evans, Denver.)

members are hard-pressed to remember racial slights or problems in the larger community.

Lon died in 1940, leaving the ranch primarily in the hands of John and Bill, with the other children having smaller shares. Esther died four months later, "of a broken heart," as Geraldine recalled. The sad deaths of their parents seemed to bond the remaining children even more to the land and to each other. The business of ranching, at least, grew larger through the next decade.

The ranch on the Fontenelle suffered from some of the same problems that have long torn apart the West, including the legal, economic, and social issues associated with water. In the early 1950s, Wyoming senator

Gale McGee led Congress to adopt the Seedskadee Bureau of Reclamation Project, popularly known as the Fontenelle Reservoir. The project called for a dam to store irrigation water as a stimulant for farming and ranching in western Wyoming, as well as to generate cheap electricity for the area. Engineers assessed that the "perfect place" for the dam and water impound behind it was on the Stepp Ranch.

The land was legally condemned, and construction of the project was initially set to begin in the late 1950s. The process dragged along until, in 1959, after much legal wrangling, the federal government offered more than $140,000—a considerable sum then—based on the financial success of Lon Stepp's business. The Stepps did not wish to sell, and they protested to the extent of their abilities, but the weight of government authority proved overwhelming. In 1960 the Stepp Ranch and its mighty grove of trees disappeared under the rising waters of the new reservoir.

＊ ＊ ＊

Full-time black ranchers in Wyoming are, in 2009, virtually nonexistent.[11] In the late 1800s Wyoming counted approximately 3 percent of its population as "black, negro or mulatto"—and 95 percent of that minuscule number lived in or around one city, Cheyenne. More than one hundred years later, the state's population is approximately 3 percent black, and 95 percent of that population lives in or around one city, Cheyenne, which is nearly four hundred miles east of the Fontenelle.

However, significance is not always measured by what can be easily seen. The quiet waters of the reservoir may obscure what lies below, but the legacy of a group of tough and tender men and women who once lived there remains a part of our combined heritage as a nation—black, white, or any color. And our society is indebted to families and individuals who have gone before. Whether we are African American or not, we should be proud that a young man and his ex-slave father brought their wives to the "Wild West" and turned a small pocket of poor soil and less water into a home, raising children and finding happiness.

❖ 10 ❖

To the Coast

CALIFORNIA

CALIFORNIA'S long and varied history incorporates the experiences of African Americans who ventured into the Golden State from its days as part of the Spanish domain to its rowdy gold rush era and through the "cowboy kingdom" years of the early twentieth century.

"California or bust (by gum)" fever carried across racial and economic lines. By 1850, when California was granted statehood, black men, women, and children numbered about two thousand out of a population of ninety-three thousand. By the turn of the twentieth century, blacks owned about fifteen hundred farms throughout California.

California joined the Union as a free state, creating legal problems for those who had retained their status as slaves because they had entered the state prior to 1850. The new state constitution did not address the issue, although early legislation discriminated severely and specifically against Mexicans, Asians, and African Americans.

Before the Civil War, about one thousand slaves lived in California. During the 1850s the state's legal system proved inconsistent when it came to either enforcing the southern laws of slavery or allowing African Americans to gain their freedom. Eventually, California passed its own fugitive slave law, which stated that anyone who entered the state either as a runaway or with his or her master prior to the state's joining the Union in 1850 was, indeed, mere property. Given the varied interpretations of the law by the courts, de facto slavery continued in California despite state laws. Nonetheless, many freedmen chose to stay and send money back home to buy out the indentures of family members and friends.

Unidentified travelers whose slogan was "California by Gum,"
circa 1890–1892, in Weaverville, California. Note the weapons worn and
carried by the driver, an indication of uneasy times.

(Photograph by William Wax. Courtesy of Peter Palmquist, Arvata, California.)

Spanish Flat, California, 1852.
Northwest of Sacramento
lay some of the richest gold-
bearing soils in North America.
California's forty-niners were
of every possible physical
description and age. The black
man may have been a slave to
the man standing next to him.

(Courtesy of the California
State Library, Sacramento.)

Alvin Coffey, California pioneer.
(Courtesy of the Northern California Center for Afro-American History Museum, Oakland.)

Photograph of a prospector, looking
for the Mother Lode in the California goldfields, circa 1855.

(Courtesy of the California State
Library, Sacramento.)

HEAD OF AUBURN RAVINE, 1852

Mining in northern California, mid-1850s. Asians and
African Americans were common laborers in the goldfields.

(Courtesy of the California State Library, Sacramento.)

One of the unwritten laws upheld by gold miners was that if a person discovered gold, it was that person's property. But if a slave discovered gold while prospecting, his master claimed ownership. Some prospectors—those without "helpers" who considered this violation of the "law" unfair—joined forces and made slave owners move out of the area. Simultaneously, and inconsistently, whites declared any claims filed by African Americans invalid.

Many blacks left the state because of widespread discrimination. Some moved to British Columbia and areas around Vancouver Island. In fact, so many left that San Francisco newspapers ran editorials criticizing punitive legislation and encouraged the emigrants to return to the state.[1] Most did not.

Alvin Coffey, born a slave, accompanied his master to the northern California goldfields in 1849. Coffey, like many other slaves, purchased his freedom with the yellow grains he sluiced from the streams and mined from the hills.

Beyond the Goldfields

The needs of the manual labor market in California attracted many black workers. Some found employment as domestics or field hands on farms in central California. Blacks also found work on the railroads, on ships, and in hotels. There were bandits and bad men, but people also raised families and prospered.

Although it is generally held that Thomas Bradley, elected in the 1980s, was the first African American mayor of the largest city west of New York City, Fernando Reyes actually holds that distinction. Reyes's family continued to own property in southern California until the mid-twentieth century.

"Lucky Baldwin's Thoroughbreds ... imported from the South in 1886."
These people were workers for the new agricultural industry in northern California.

(Courtesy of the California State Library, Sacramento.)

Railroad workers, circa 1890. Known as "gandy dancers,"
these men constructed railbeds, set the ties, and laid the rails.

(Courtesy of the City of Oakland, California.)

William Shorrey, a sailor, businessman, and owner of a fleet of coastal shipping and package-delivery vessels that serviced the West Coast of the United States as far north as Alaska.

(Courtesy of the Northern California Center for Afro-American History Museum, Oakland.)

Employees of the Palace Hotel, San Francisco, circa 1890.

(Courtesy of the California State Library, Sacramento.)

Charlie Rodriguez was born in Jamaica. He concentrated his activities in the Santa Cruz area in the mid-1800s, ultimately serving three terms in San Quentin State Prison.

(Courtesy of the Miriam Matthews Collection, California African-American Museum, Los Angeles.)

Colonel Allen Allensworth, whose work in the military of the town that now bears his name led the nation in—among other things— establishing a system that allowed soldiers to further their education while on active duty.

(Courtesy of the California State Archives, Sacramento.)

Dr. and Mrs. Monroe. He was a physician in Los Angeles, circa 1900.
By the late 1800s, occupations that had been denied most African Americans
became more accessible, as did the social positions that came with them.

(Courtesy of the Miriam Matthews Collection, California African-American Museum, Los Angeles.)

Juan Fernando Reyes, circa
1880, the first black mayor
of Los Angeles. His racial
heritage was Mexican and
African American. He ruled the
burgeoning pueblo in the late
part of the nineteenth century.

(Courtesy of the Miriam Matthews
Collection, California African-
American Museum, Los Angeles.)

❋ 11 ❋

Alaska and the
Pacific Northwest

Already Alaska beckons on the north, and pointing
to her wealth of natural resources asks the nation on
what new terms the new age will deal with her.

— Frederick Jackson Turner,
The Frontier in American History

ALASKA

IN THE LATE NINETEENTH CENTURY, tales of gold and riches in Alaska attracted a multitude of people to some of the most forbidding land on earth. Among those who flocked to Alaska were miners, gamblers, trappers, freight haulers, whalers, entrepreneurs, sailors, soldiers, cooks, and prostitutes.

Most likely, Canadians were the early migrants to the Northwest territories and "Seward's folly," as Alaska was often called. Although an 1880 census of primarily southern Alaska found no African Americans, the first known African American to appear on an official list was James Walker in Sitka in October 1870. He was noted as "male, Negro, aged 25." Apparently born in Panama, Walker worked as a cook and was married to Maria, a woman whose racial background was unlisted but who had been born in Sitka.[1]

By 1890 records indicate that 112 blacks resided in Alaska. Apparently, most worked in the whaling business and lived in places as remote and disparate as Cape Smythe, Point Barrow, and Port Clarence.

Nome, Alaska, during the gold rush. Note the unidentified African American on the left.

(Courtesy of the Anchorage Museum of History and Art, Alaska.)

WHALING

The days of great whaling ships began with hearty adventurers and businessmen out of New Bedford, Massachusetts, and other whaling ports along the eastern seaboard. Primarily sailing the Atlantic, Pacific, and Indian oceans hunting the gigantic marine mammals, mariners spent upwards of eight months at a time at sea, returning only when weather or overloaded holds forced a return to home port for a respite of a few weeks. In Alaska, however, the whaling procedure differed. Since crews spent several months sailing from the East to their destinations on the northwestern coast, there was little profit in sailing all the way back around the tip

U.S. revenue cutter, the *Bear*. Its most famous captain was Michael Healy, an African American whose deeds are well remembered in the sailing history of that region.

Michael "Mad Mike" Healy (*on the right*), captain of the *Bear*, with his crew. He commanded the ship from 1886 to 1896. Not as well recorded were his shorter commands of the ships *McCullock* (1900) and *Thelis* (1902–1903).

(Courtesy of the Rasmussen Collection, University of Alaska Archives, Fairbanks.)

Whaling crew, Alaska, circa 1890. Men came from New England,
Europe, the Cape Verde Islands, Tonga, Samoa, and elsewhere for work on
whaling ships in the Pacific Ocean and Bering Straits.

(Courtesy of the Rasmussen Collection, University of Alaska Archives, Fairbanks.)

of South America to return home. Instead, crews stayed over the winter
months in harbors such as those near Barrow and Hope on the northern
coast, sailing south only to transfer their loads. By staying as late as possible prior to the onset of winter, crews harvested a large number of whales,
although rapidly forming ice floes destroyed both men and ships if they
stayed too long.

Michael "Mad Mike" Healy, a light-skinned black man who sailed the
Bear in Alaskan waters for several years, developed into perhaps the best-
known captain of any U.S. revenue cutter. Although skilled in his trade, he
also possessed a violent temper and a penchant for mistreating his crew.
Healy faced charges more than once for poor leadership, but his connections proved influential in sustaining his rank and tenure. Under his
captaincy, the *Bear* became one of the best-known revenue cutters of its
time, and the most photographed. Many African Americans served under
Healy's command.[2]

An African American crew of a whaling ship, lined up for an informal portrait. By the time the American whaling trade ended, more than 90 percent of the crews were African American.

(Courtesy of the Providence Public Library Archives, Rhode Island.)

Many dark-skinned crew hailed from the South Sea islands, as had the fictional Queequeg, a main character in Herman Melville's *Moby Dick*.[3] At first, few New Englanders worked aboard the whaling ships; eventually, over the years, they grew into the majority.

The story of one of the black men who worked in the days of sail is worth mentioning here. Born in 1902 in New Bedford, Massachusetts, Ernest Johnson grew up in the shadow of the tall ships based there in the late days of the whaling trade.[4] Although not from a whaling family, he longed to join the crews of the vessels that sailed to exotic lands. He would, of course, learn that the trade was filled with danger and boredom when he became one of the many men of dark skin who chased great whales in the warm waters of the South Atlantic Ocean.

While his family thought he was in town training as a typewriter repairman, he actually spent his days near the anchored whaling ships,

Ernest Johnson, circa 1980. Photographed when
Mr. Johnson was nearing his seventieth birthday.

(Courtesy of Ernest Johnson, Cleveland, Ohio.)

talking with the men about their jobs and lives. Too young to sign on as
a crewmate, the fourteen-year-old Johnson forged a note from his aunt
that allowed him to join the roster of the *A. M. Nicholson* under the alias
"Ernest H. Rosa." He eventually spent twenty-six years sailing on all the
major seas of the world.

GOLD RUSH

The Alaska gold rush began in 1896 with the discovery of gold in the
Klondike. Thousands poured northward from Washington and Idaho
through British Columbia, while others came by ship up the Inland Passage out of Seattle to ports in Sitka, Nome, Dawson, Ketchikan, and Skagway. Many blacks were among these numbers. In the boomtown of Dawson, for example, there was St. John Atherton, who uncovered some thirty
thousand dollars worth of gold.

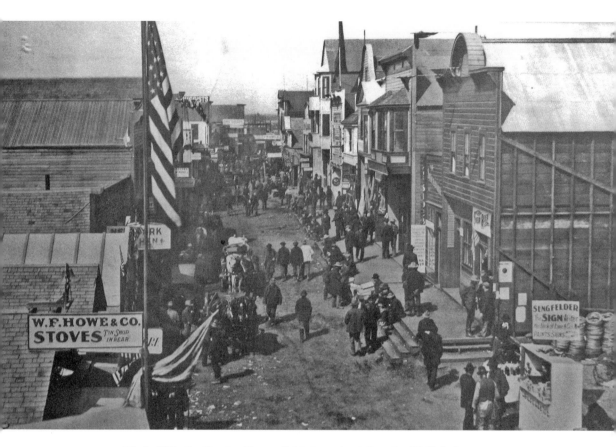

Marked "On the Streets of Juneau," this image is attributed to W. H. Jackson.

Other Dawson residents included the Black Prince, a prizefighter; ex-slave Arthur Jordan, a cook who became a well-known man-about-town; and a Mrs. Mason, an African American laundrywoman who made a small fortune serving miners' needs—and then lost it to Jefferson Randolph "Soapy" Smith II, an infamous white con man from Texas. Other blacks who ventured to Alaska included Black Alice, who made her fortune in Nome; Leonard Seppala, who raced dogsleds near Nome; and a woman called Black Kitty, who practiced the world's oldest profession in the Klondike.

WASHINGTON AND OREGON

Records of black pioneers in the Northwest date from the late 1700s when traders recognized the value of the area's fur trade. Marcus Lopez, a Cape Verdean who was a crewmate on Captain Robert Gray's *Lady Washington*

Miners at the base of Chilkoot Pass, waiting their turn for the twenty-mile climb into the northern regions of the territory. Note the African American man (*hands on hips*), center left.

(Courtesy of the Alaska State Archives, Juneau.)

The Twenty-fourth Infantry at Skagway.
The soldiers were stationed at several places in the territory.

(Courtesy of the National Park Service, Anchorage.)

(which sailed from Boston to the northwest coast in 1787 to load furs), was likely the first African American to step onto the shores of the Pacific Northwest. York, an African American who was with the Lewis and Clark expedition, arrived on the coast approximately fifteen years later.

Few black settlers found their way to the Northwest while slavery was still practiced in the South. By the mid-1800s, however, a few had followed the Oregon Trail northwestward. After seven months on the trail, for example, George Bush and a few hardy colleagues made their way to The Dalles, south of the Columbia River. Bush, a freeman in his native Pennsylvania, served as the community's leader. A successful farmer, he also purchased a ship, the *Orbit,* and traded lumber in West Coast ports. In 1889, his son, William Owen Bush, became a member of Washington's first legislature, which established the state's college of agriculture, later to become Washington State University, in Pullman.

Sketch of George Bush.

(Courtesy of Ralph Hayes, Seattle.)

George Washington, circa 1870.

(Courtesy of the Oregon
Historical Society, Portland.)

George Washington.

(Courtesy of the Lewis County Historical Museum, Chehalis, Washington.)

Mary Jane Cooness, first wife
of George Washington.

(Courtesy of the Lewis and Clark Historical
Museum, Chehalis, Washington.)

Canyon City, Oregon, circa 1860. When gold rush fever spread
northward from California, rugged miners moved with it. These
men prospected around Canyon City in the mid-1860s.

(Courtesy of the Grant City Museum, Canyon City, Oregon.)

In 1850 a black boy named George Washington migrated westward along the Oregon Trail with the white family that had adopted him. Years later, in 1872, he heard that the Northern Pacific Railroad was laying tracks across Washington Territory. Seizing the initiative, Washington platted a town, Centerville, and started advertising the lots he had set aside for sale. The town was renamed Centralia and became prosperous, surviving the panic of 1873 when Washington used his own money to provide food for the community and help it change from a logging industry to a more diversified economy.

ROSLYN, WASHINGTON

The small community of Roslyn—noted today more for its verdant beauty and movie and television location sites than for its connection to black western history—is tucked away in forested mountains one hundred miles east of Seattle. Founded as a coal mining town by the Oregon-Washington Improvement Company, it existed as a white community from its beginnings until the day in 1888 when miners walked out for higher wages and improved working conditions. The so-called Northern Pacific coal strike resulted in several deaths and, quite unintentionally, a radical change in the ethnography of the area, when the coal company decided not to negotiate with striking miners. Instead, recruiters fanned out across the southern states to locate black men willing to relocate to the far reaches of the Pacific Northwest to work in the mines. Many young men jumped at the chance, and some brought wives and families with them. It was not until they were actually en route, in coach cars, that many learned they were going to be strikebreakers. Most stayed on the train and relocated in Roslyn. Once there, they endured catcalls and racial slurs yet ultimately persevered. Over the period of a decade, Roslyn transformed into a predominantly black community. African American families such as the Donaldsons, Smalleys, Darks, Ammonnettes (all of whom came to Roslyn during its mining days) and others whose names are lost to history built the foundation of a thriving community that lasted until the 1930s.

The range of African American pioneering in what demographers often call the "empty quarter" of the United States was as varied as anywhere else, but the number of pioneers was fewer. Still, individuals and families who moved to the Northwest in the late 1800s and early 1900s formed the basis of today's populations. ⚜

Lucille and John Breckenridge, Roslyn, Washington, circa 1898. Lucy Breckenridge
and her son John arrived in Roslyn with the strikebreakers in 1888. Accompanying
Lucy from Virginia were her husband, Henry, and Mary Perkins, Henry's sister.

(Courtesy of the Spokane Northwest Black Pioneers, Washington.)

Schoolchildren in Roslyn, circa 1890.

(Courtesy of the Roslyn Museum, Roslyn, Washington.)

Spokane's first African American police officer, Henry W. Sample,
who served from 1892 to 1895, with his favorite horse.

(Courtesy of the Spokane Public library, Washington.)

Big-timber loggers worked in the virgin forests of Idaho in the late 1800s. Joe, Roy, and Chuck Wells, along with an unidentified white man, are the lumberjacks in this picture.

(Courtesy of the Latah County Historical Society, Moscow, Idaho.)

Joe and Lou Wells, circa 1888.

(Courtesy of the Latah County Historical Society, Moscow, Idaho.)

❈ 12 ❈

"Haole 'Ele 'Ele" in Owhyhee

THE SANDWICH ISLANDS are twenty-six hundred miles from the western shores of the United States. Economics, political interests, changing population patterns, and a growing sea trade reduced the psychological distance to a manageable barrier for both black and white entrepreneurs in the nineteenth century.[1]

By the time the British sailing captain James Cook landed his expedition on the beaches of Oahu in 1778, other nations were also extending their spheres of influence throughout that part of the world. Stories about Cook's exploits filtered back to the European continent and were the apparent source of foreign interest in these exotic new lands. Many nations sent sailing ships to the islands, and today their crews' descendants

Whaling in the South Seas. This segment of an oil-on-canvas painting was probably
done by a crewman. It shows a whaling boat from the *Uncas* on its initial trip
to the Sandwich Islands, circa 1868. Note the racial diversity of the crew.

Members of King Kamehameha's naval guard, circa 1900.
(Courtesy of the Hawaii State Archives, Honolulu.)

make up a large segment of the island chain's non-Polynesian population. The islands (later known as "Owhyhee" and, in the nineteenth century, as "Hawaii") attracted foreigner investors, sailors, businessmen, missionaries, and others, including an unknown number of African Americans.

Anthony Allen, a fugitive slave from "German Flats" (probably Schenectady), New York, arrived in Oahu around 1810 and set up shop near Waikiki Beach—the first recorded African American entrepreneur in the Hawaiian Islands. There are no verifiable paintings or other images of Allen, but his influence extended throughout the area. Owner of a bar, a boardinghouse, and a bowling alley,[2] he also established a neighborhood hospital, started a small truck farm, and ran a "house of entertainment" that catered to sailors. Allen became a popular figure with visiting dignitaries and politicians. He married a Hawaiian woman and lived out his years enjoying his island-centered fame until his death around 1835.

Kamehameha the Great, who designated Allen his "trusted adviser," welcomed African American immigrants to his kingdom.[3] By the 1840s, Hawaiian society included black military and royal aides. George H. Hyatt, an escaped slave, conducted the royal band from 1845 to 1848.

In the early 1840s, many African Americans lived in Honolulu, including Charles H. Nicholson. He built a prosperous tailor shop and was

Young Portuguese or Jamaican woman, photographed in Hawaii, circa 1890.
References to Portugal often carried the connotation of "black" in early days, since
the Cape Verde Islands, lying west of Africa, were a Portuguese colony. For many,
this woman typified the mixed racial heritage of one subgroup of Hawaiian society.

(Courtesy of the Bishop Museum, Honolulu.)

Flensing a whale as it is hoisted aboard a ship.
(Courtesy of the Providence Public Library Archives, Rhode Island.)

well known for his congeniality, his all-linen suits, and the white adobe building that housed his business for nearly twenty years.[4] Local lore indicates that because of the color of his skin he was not buried in consecrated ground, and the location of his grave remains unknown. However, his wife and son—half Hawaiian, half black—suffered no such discrimination, and their graves are well marked in Kawaiahao Cemetery.

Hawaii's population grew dramatically as immigrants arrived, lured by the money one could earn in the sea trades of commerce and whaling and in sugarcane and pineapple farming. Throughout the mid-1800s, small shops and service industries blossomed, and commercial centers developed into cities and towns. In short order, white missionaries, Chinese and Japanese laborers, Koreans, Filipinos, Polynesians, Portuguese,

A young man with his banjo, an instrument derived from
the stringed musical devices brought from Africa by slaves.

Jews, Lutherans, Mormons, and others arrived, creating one of the most
dynamic and polyglot societies in the world.

The whaling industry, which flourished in the northeastern United
States from the 1700s until the 1920s, employed substantial numbers of
black sailors. Most of them hailed from Portuguese West Africa (today,
Senegal and the Cape Verde Islands).

West African men brought stringed instruments, later to be called
"banjos," with them to the Americas. This instrument made the perfect
musical companion to the Portuguese "squeeze box," or accordion. The
two provided the standard backup for chanteys sung by crewmen as they
sailed the seven seas.

In 1811 Steven Francis, a black cook on the whaling ship the *New Haz-
ard,* jumped ship in Oahu and joined the hundreds of others who had similarly chosen a new way of life on dry land.[5] Local newspapers reported an
influx of new citizens in 1818, former sailors from ships such as the *Columbia, Santa Rosa,* and *Argentina.* In 1836, the American whaler *Chelsea* lost
10 percent of its crew in one evening from desertion. Black crew members
such as David Pine, Thomas Johnson, John Wilson, Elyners Case, and
Lewis Temple jumped ship in Hawaii during the mid-1800s and added to
the population of the island.[6]

Betsy Stockton arrived in Hawaii in the early 1800s and began a long career in church service and teaching in the islands and, later, back on the mainland.

(Courtesy of the Mission House Museum Library, Honolulu.)

Several dozen black missionaries journeyed to the Hawaiian Islands in the nineteenth century, but virtually none of them stayed or can be traced to anyone in today's island population.[7] White missionaries from the Church of Jesus Christ of Latter-day Saints (Mormons) and the Presbyterian Church demonstrated their religious zeal to convert the islanders. For example, Presbyterian missionary Charles Stewart brought his family to Maui in 1823 and opened the Sandwich Island Mission in Lahaina. A black woman named Betsy Stockton came with him.

Born a slave to Major Robert Stockton in Princeton, New Jersey, later freed by the Stockton family, she was described as "precocious and bright" and quickly learned the Hawaiian language, which she used in her fiery sermonizing. She impressed the Reverend Stewart and all who witnessed her zeal for Christianity.[8] In short order she set up a school in Lahaina to teach children. She did not stay long, however, leaving the islands with Stewart in 1825. In succeeding years, Stockton led a movement to form the First Presbyterian Church of Colour in Princeton, New Jersey, which was renamed the Witherspoon Street Church in 1848. Her life was devoted to teaching—in Philadelphia, briefly in Canada, and for thirty years in Princeton, where she died in 1865.

In 1875 T. McCants Stewart, a freeborn African American from Charleston, South Carolina, earned a law degree from Howard University in Washington, D.C. After working as a journalist in New York City,

Carlotta Stewart (shown circa 1900) graduated from Hawaiian schools.
Her teaching and administrative careers, both in the islands and
on the mainland, led to inclusion in Hawaiian society and fame.

(Courtesy of the Moorland-Spingarn Research Collection, Howard University, Washington, D.C.)

Antoine DeSant, a Cape Verde whaler, ship's captain, frigate pilot, and California gold miner, whose family dedicated their lives to the sea. He often commanded his ships in the waters of the Hawaiian Islands, and subsequently became prosperous and influential in American sailing trades.

(Courtesy of the Mystic Seaport Museum, Connecticut.)

Pineapple field hands, Hawaiian Islands, circa 1880. This stereograph shows African American workers during the short-lived practice of recruiting men from the southern States.

(Courtesy of the Hawaii State Archives, Honolulu.)

he emigrated to Liberia as part of the Back-to-Africa movement. Later, in 1898, Stewart and his daughter Carlotta sailed to Hawaii. Carlotta Stewart graduated from Oahu College (Punahou School) with a degree in teaching, a profession she practiced in the islands until 1924. She was the principal of a multicultural elementary school, becoming a well-known figure in middle-class Hawaiian society.

In the early 1900s, the all-black Twenty-fifth Infantry relocated to bases near Honolulu. Additional African American servicemen from other units soon followed. Large-scale farming after the turn of the century attracted black workers from the mainland.

The black population of Hawaii at the end of the twentieth century numbered approximately eighteen thousand, located mainly on Oahu. Hawaii, with its reputation for opportunities and its exotic climate, continues to attract individuals with differing ethnic and racial heritages, including blacks.

❧ 13 ❧

Follow the Drinkin' Gourd

Follow the drinkin' gourd,
For the old man is a-waitin'
For to carry you to freedom,
Follow the drinkin' gourd.
Now the river bank'll make a mighty good road
The dead trees will show you the way
Left foot, peg foot, travelin' on
Follow the drinkin' gourd.

—A traditional song

MOST RESIDENTS of the United States assume that Canada's historical involvement in black issues has been minimal. In a counterassumption, many Canadians think Americans see blacks only in warm, southerly climes. As with so many preconceptions about blacks, both of these views are incorrect.

THE EARLY HISTORY OF BLACKS IN CANADA

In 1619 a Dutchman sold twenty slaves in Jamestown, Virginia. By the mid-1600s black slaves were routinely bought and sold in Quebec. The first recorded slave sale in Canada was in 1628, when Olivier la Jeune was purchased.

In 1685 the Code Noir legalized slavery in New France. Competition from the slaveholding British colonies had forced the French king's decision. By 1759, 3,604 slaves lived in New France, of whom about 1,100 were blacks.

"Heading North," a popular lithograph of the Underground Railroad period. As the lyrics to the song indicate, heading north, toward the Big Dipper, was both a real and allegorical solution to problems of slavery.

"Negresses Selling Mayflowers on the Market Place" is the title of a woodcut from *Canadian Illustrated News*, May 5, 1872. The early illustrated newspapers were as popular in Canada as were *Harper's Weekly* and *Leslie's Illustrated Newspaper* in the United States.

(Sketch by W. O. Carlisle, *Canadian Illustrated News*, 1872.)

The "peculiar institution" as practiced north of the border differed somewhat from slavery in the American colonies to the south. Without a plantation system in a hot, humid climate, many Canadian slaves faced less rigorous work generally; they did not endure forced labor as did their counterparts to the south.

After both the American Revolution and the War of 1812, more than 42,000 black people fled to Canada, seeking refuge. The British government offered freedom to blacks in return for their pledges of fealty to the Crown. As a result, some 5,000 left Georgia in 1782, and the next year more than 3,000 sailed from South Carolina after the Treaty of Paris was signed.

In 1793 Lieutenant Governor Colonel John Graves Simcoe introduced a bill to prevent the further importation of slaves into upper Canada and to free the children of slaves living in Canada when they reached the age of twenty-five. To American blacks, the nation to the north emerged as the promised land. Almost immediately, large numbers of blacks began heading for Canada, following the Big Dipper in the Ursa Major constellation; a line drawn from the two stars at the right end of the Big Dipper's bowl leads north to Polaris, the guiding North Star. As the song proclaimed, they followed "the drinkin' gourd."

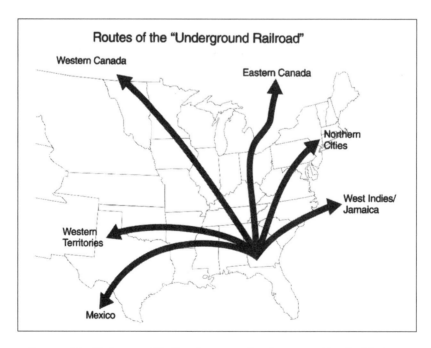

Routes of the Underground Railroad: western Canada, eastern Canada, Mexico.

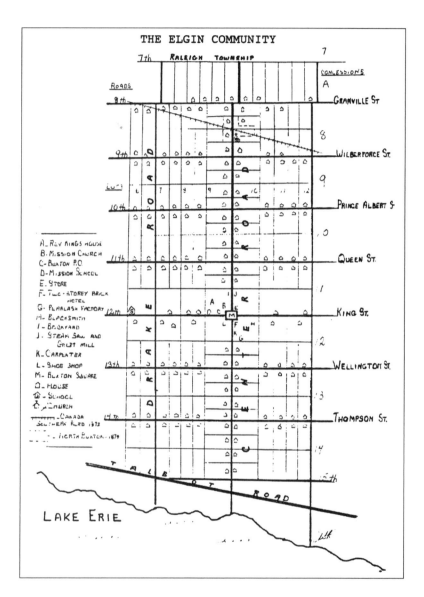

The Elgin community, North Buxton, Ontario. No photographs of the early North Buxton Elgin community exist, but this town map hints at its size and complexity.

(Courtesy of the Raleigh Township Memorial Museum, North Buxton, Ontario.)

Amor de Cosmos, born William Alexander Smith in Nova Scotia in 1815. This mixed-race man was a gold prospector in California, a businessman, and a newspaperman who eventually became a powerful political figure who defended the union of British Columbia and Vancouver Island, thus bringing British Columbia into the new Canadian confederation. He then served in the second premiership of the province.

(Courtesy of the City of Vancouver Archives, British Columbia; Out. p. 815, Neg. 373.)

In the 1820s and 1830s American abolitionists and their religious supporters provided a well-organized system of escape routes to Mexico, the Bahamas, and—on the invisible wheels of the Underground Railroad—to Canada, to towns such as Chatham, St. Catherines, Blenheim, Owen Sound, and Amherstberg, in Ontario.[1]

In August 1833 William IV of Britain outlawed the practice of slavery, making Canada an even more desirable destination for American blacks. Sympathetic abolitionists in America and many Canadians participated in the effort to move escaped slaves via the Underground Railroad, and thousands of black men, women, and children followed this route to freedom in Ontario and Quebec.

The Underground Railroad offered several final destination points, but one of the most important—and long-lasting—settlements was at Elgin, later North Buxton, Ontario. Located on a fertile plain in Raleigh Township, the village was established in 1849. In short order, the town grew to approximately fifteen hundred individuals, virtually all of them runaway slaves from the States.

Unlike many other settlements of this type, Elgin boasted a strong economy, based on booming agricultural production plus the added stability of permanent employment with the Trans-Canadian Railway. The latter allowed workers to purchase land and turn homesteads into permanent family residences.

By the 1850s the black population of Ontario had reached seventy-five thousand, amounting to approximately 8 percent of Ontario's population. In those same years, the first newspapers for black readers began to be published by blacks in Canada, including Henry Bibb's *Voice of the Fugitive* and the *Provincial Freeman,* edited by Mary Ann Shadd.

❖ ❖ ❖

African Canadian pioneers established a pattern for the thousands of like-minded individuals who moved to Canada after them. A few of their stories follow.

Matthew Da Costa, a mulatto, early explorer, linguist, and pioneer, left his home of La Rochelle in Quebec in 1606 to serve as interpreter of Indian languages for Samuel de Champlain (the Father of Canada). The 1606 Poutrincourt-Champlain expedition explored Nova Scotia, where Da Costa became a founding member of one of Canada's oldest fraternal clubs, the Order of Good Cheer.

John Baker, born a slave in Quebec, fought in many battles in Canada in the 1700s. He joined Wellington's forces at the Battle of Waterloo.

Another Canadian pioneer of African descent, Colonel Stephen Blucke, led colonial "black pioneers" who fought for the British in the American Revolution. Along with the Maroons, he left for Nova Scotia, where he became a social leader and entertained Prince William Henry, later King William IV, on his visit to the new land.[2]

Circa 1820, Dan Williams, from the United States, arrived in western Alberta to work the gold claims and serve as a "cook, trapper, vagrant, idler, or squatter, as chance suited him."[3] He befriended and worked with early explorers of the Peace River Country in Alberta. Notably, Williams sued the Hudson's Bay Company over land it expropriated from him to build a new outpost. Williams protested that his "squatter's rights" superseded those of the company. He engaged gunmen hired by the company in a pistol fight, resulting in his arrest. At trial, the court found Williams innocent of attempted murder and upheld his claim to the property—a rare instance of the Hudson's Bay Company losing a legal case. Williams

Miners on Dominion Creek in British Columbia, circa 1880.
The gold rush lured many Americans northward in the latter half of the
nineteenth century. Among them were black men and women.

(Courtesy of the Rasmussen Collection, University of Alaska Archives, Fairbanks.)

returned to prospecting and selling vegetables to other miners. Never a
slave in Canada, Williams uniquely embraced his new citizenship status,
often posting signs on his property declaring his loyalty to no one but the
queen of England.[4] He died in July 1887.

Martin R. Delaney, an explorer and one of the first black majors in
the U.S. Army, spent most of his life arguing that black men and women
needed black leaders. Also known as one of the first black nationalists, Delaney left the States at various times between 1856 and 1861, living for a time
in Chatham, Ontario, near the northern terminus of the Underground
Railroad in Canada, and traveling to Liberia in 1860. But he returned to
the United States during the Civil War to actively recruit black soldiers.
He met Abraham Lincoln early in 1865, and in February of that year he was
commissioned as the first black field officer in the Union army.

Medical men of African descent who fought in the Civil War included doctors Anderson Rufin Abbott and Alexander T. Augusta. Born in Toronto in 1837, Abbott studied medicine at the University of Toronto and later served as a surgeon in the Union army. Augusta hailed from Virginia and later became Canada's first noted doctor. He studied medicine at Trinity College, University of Toronto. He also served in the Civil War as a major and as a surgeon to the Seventh U.S. Colored Troops. He left the service as a lieutenant colonel.

James Douglas was born in Demerara, British Guiana, the illegitimate son of John Douglas, a Scottish merchant, and a Creole woman of mixed European and African heritage, possibly Martha Ann Ritchie or Miss Ritchie. At an early age his father took him to Scotland, where he was educated at Lanark. He went to Canada as a young man and was an employee of the Hudson's Bay Company. He married a young woman of Irish and Indian heritage and became a political leader, eventually serving as governor of Vancouver Island and the British Columbia colony.

Noted for his ability to communicate effectively with native Indians as well as the newcomers, he was popular and effective. As a way to combat the large numbers of Americans flooding north into British Columbia in search of gold, who he feared would eventually force the annexation of the colony to the United States, Douglas advertised in California, encouraging African Americans to move north to British Columbia and become British subjects. Hundreds of "black pioneers" responded.

Records from 1873 indicate that the Cassiar region of British Columbia hosted thousands of prospectors during the gold rush years, prior to the richer discoveries in Alaska. Some three hundred Chinese and fifty black miners worked that area, and one by the name of McDame struck gold on Dease Creek. Miners called the camp "McDame," in his honor.

"Hundreds of thousands of pioneers from the Middle West have crossed the national boundary into Canadian wheat fields eager to find farms for their children," historian Frederick Jackson Turner wrote.[5] The saga of the Blakey family is recorded earlier in this volume. Other members of the Blakey family also moved to the western United States, drawn by promises of rich farmland and a freedom that they had never experienced. However, when they reached South Dakota, they quickly moved on to Athabasca Landing, Junkins (Wildwood), Alberta, now called Amber Valley.

Martha Jane "Mattie" Mayes also found the lure of Canada's prairies irresistible. She was born a slave on the Jesse Partridge plantation near

The Victoria pioneer rifle corps ("African Rifles"), an all-black
defensive force, the first in British Columbia, formed by Governor James
Douglas and the Hudson's Bay Company in 1860.

(Courtesy of the City of Vancouver Archives, British Columbia; Mil-P. 79, Neg. 68.)

James Douglas, a mixed-race man born in the West Indies, being sworn in as the
first governor of British Columbia, November 19, 1858. Along with the "Victoria
Rifles," in 1851 he would also form the "Voltigeurs," a French-speaking, mixed-
race group that was the predecessor of the Victoria Police Department.

The Gazetteer and Guide

A MONTHLY MAGAZINE.

JAMES A. ROSS, *25/4/03* EDITOR AND MANAGER.
J. H. LYNCH. ADVERTISING MANAGER.

OFFICE OF PUBLICATION, 183 CLINTON STREET, BUFFALO, N. Y.

BRANCHES: *Pittsburg, Philadelphia Montreal, New York City, Cleveland, Chicago, St. Louis, St. Paul, Toronto, Omaha and Portland, Ore.*

An Opportunity for the Negro in Western Canada.

No better opportunity affords itself to the a ricultural Negro than in Western Canada. And more especially those who live in the Southland and have a little capital. The one salvation of the Negro is to mirate to a section where he can be a component part in building up an undeveloped country under favorable conditions, there is no question to the fact, that it was largely the Negro labor that built up the Southland.' In this section of the country the farm hands are in demand land is cheap, and productive, the present indications are that it is unsafe for the Negro to continue to purchase property in the Southland. It is in our opinion a desperate chance to continue there deposits in the banks of that section. With a good strong arm a man can go to this section of Canada and in two years he can make enough money to send for his family, besides they can engage in agricultural pursuits taking up free grant lands, buying railway bonds or purchasing the improved farms to be found in advantageous positions in every province; or in mining they can secure employment in the manufacturing industries; or, if possessed of a settled income, living will be found to be much cheaper in Canada with the benefits of a fine, healthy climate, magnificent scenery, abundant opportunities for investments, and facilities for education and placing children in life not to be excelled any where; that is, those who have agricultural experience can succeed without doubt.

MORE NEGROES COMING TO SETTLE IN ALBERTA

Twenty More Farmers Are On the Way to Join the Colony

Lethbridge *12/4/11*

Guthrie. Okla., April 11.—The exodus of negroes from this state to Alberta which started several months ago, is continuing, despite the fact that it is not being encouraged by the Canadian government. Twenty negro farmers from near Fallis, Lincoln county, left here last night to join the colony in Alberta. They expect to take claims and immediately build homes and start their crops, after which their families, numbering in all about two hundred persons, will join them. It is said here that a colonization company is financing the negroes during the first ——

GENERAL EXODUS OF NEGROES INTO CANADA

Movement Follows Colonizing Campaign by Canadian Representatives During Winter Months.

OKLAHOMA CITY, March 26.—The final action of the Canadian government in admitting to that country negro families from Oklahoma is having the effect of further colonization movement among the negroes, especially in Okfuskee, Muskogee and Creek counties, where there is a heavy negro popoulation and several exclusive negro towns.

The first emigration to Canada during the past week was of ninety families, perhaps 500 negroes in all, from Okfuskee county. They sold all their property in this state, intending to homestead quarter section claims in Canada. Many other negroes are making preparations to start and indications are there will be a general exodus. It develops that the Canadian colonization work among the negroes has been in progress for several months, the intention being to move 1,000 families, or about 7,000 negroes, this spring, of which the Clearview emigrants formed the advance guard. It is understood a treaty provision admits them to Canada if they have $5 each in cash.

The emigrants as a rule are educated negroes, many of whom were taught in the government schools for Indians in old Indian Territory. They are leaving Oklahoma because of adverse legislation, "Jim Crow" coach and depot laws, the "grandfather clause" act that prohibits them from voting, separate school laws and others.

The Gazetteer and Guide, March 26, 1903

These articles are from the *Gazetteer and Guide Magazine,* a monthly published in New York and widely circulated among blacks in the West. Such articles alarmed those whites who thought too many African Americans were settling in Canada.

(Courtesy of the City of Vancouver Archives, British Columbia; general collection.)

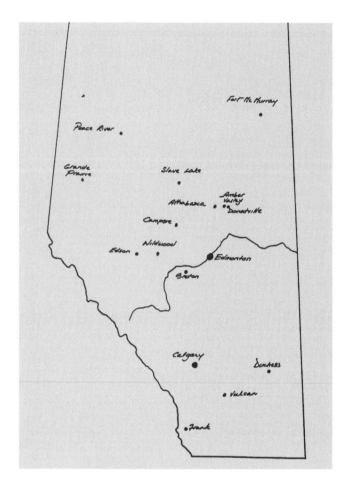

Western Alberta, Canada, circa 1890,
indicating major black settlements.

Atlanta, Georgia, around 1847, and was a young girl when her master went into hiding and left the property under the direction of Mattie's grandfather. Subsequent Civil War battles left the plantation in ruins; Partridge returned only long enough to declare the farm a failure. Emancipation and the war had destroyed him, and he left the newly freed slaves to fend for themselves. Mattie's family moved to Tennessee, where she met and married Joseph Mayes.

Some years later the young couple moved to Indian Territory and started a family. They soon grew dissatisfied, however, and began planning a northward migration after seeing a promotional advertisement for Canada. Joseph Mayes had wanted such a move, and Mattie saw the northward

Mattie Mayes, a resident of Alberta, circa 1915.

(Courtesy of the Saskatchewan Provincial Archives, Regina.)

migration as prophetic, because, in her words, "God freed us." Those heading north included Joseph, Mattie (then 52 years old), and ten children.
Taking a circuitous route through St. Paul, Minnesota, and on to Winnipeg, Regina, and Saskatoon, they made their way to Battleford, where
they filed a claim in Maidstone, in the Eldon district of Saskatchewan.

Next, by oxcart, the family journeyed to their homestead and began
farming, which they continued to do through the 1920s and 1930s. The
couple welcomed three more children to the family, which had become
the center of the Eldon settlement. Joseph died in the 1920s, but Mattie
lived until March 1953. She was 104 at the time of her death.

Abraham Shadd,
circa 1860, a political,
religious, and social
leader of the Buxton
community in Ontario.

(Courtesy of the Raleigh
Township Memorial Museum,
North Buxton, Ontario.)

The American Civil War called many of the settlers back to the States solely to fight the South. Their stories are legendary.

Abraham Doras Shadd was born a slave in 1801. He moved with his brother Absalom from Delaware to Pennsylvania in 1833. About seventeen years later the brothers relocated to Buxton, Raleigh Township, Ontario.

A close friend of the Reverend Josiah Henson (ostensibly the source of stories used in Harriet Beecher Stowe's *Uncle Tom's Cabin*), Abraham Shadd soon entered local politics, serving on the Raleigh Township Council. He met on occasion with the American abolitionist John Brown, who often visited and lectured in the area. In his spare time he established Masonic lodges throughout lower Canada.

Shadd had married Harriet Parnell before moving to Buxton; together they raised thirteen children, many of whom became influential Canadian citizens. One of their oldest children, Abraham W., returned to the States, worked as a lawyer, and served with the Northern military during the Civil War, stationed in Mississippi as a member of the Twenty-fourth Kent Militia from Canada, who were volunteers for the Union.

Abraham Shadd, circa
1885, in his Union
Army uniform.

(Courtesy of the Raleigh
Township Memorial Museum,
North Buxton, Ontario.)

Mary Shadd Cary, author,
teacher, abolitionist, journalist.

(Courtesy of the Raleigh Township Memorial
Museum, North Buxton, Ontario.)

Julius Isaac, an immigrant from Grenada, was appointed chief justice of the Federal Court of Canada, December 1991.

(Courtesy of the Caribbean Association of Manitoba, Canada.)

The Shady Creek Methodist Church, near Victoria Island, British Columbia, founded by blacks. Although there is no longer a sizable black community in the area, this church remains as an artifact of the African American experience in Canada.

Shadd rose to the rank of captain of the 104th Colored Troops, and served as an aide and clerk to Major Martin R. Delaney.

The eldest of the senior Abraham's children, Mary Ann Camberton Shadd, was born when the family was living free in Wilmington, Delaware. The family was deeply involved in the Underground Railroad, an experience that would shape Mary's life. When she was ten, she moved with her family to West Chester, Pennsylvania, near Philadelphia, and attended a Quaker school. Abraham had joined the Society of Friends when he became active in the National Convention for the Improvement of Free People of Color in the United States and the American Anti-slavery Society.

Mary grew up in an environment of abolitionist sentiment, led and fueled by her father and his friends, all of whom subscribed to William Lloyd Garrison's *Liberator*—a newspaper so strong in its views that in many cities black people (free, in name only) were forbidden by law to carry it from the post office. In the December 29, 1865, issue, for example, Garrison wrote, "What of the four millions of colored people in the entire south?... The American Government is but a mockery and deserves to be overthrown, if they are to be left without protection, as sheep in the midst of wolves.... Let the edict go forth, trumpet-tongued, that there shall be a speedy end put to this bloody misrule."

The murder of Elijah P. Lovejoy, editor and pioneering antislavery writer in Alton, Illinois, had a profound impact on Mary, her family, and the community. Lovejoy was a family friend and a founding member of the Anti-slavery Society. His death, clearly a catalytic event in Mary's life, turned her toward careers in teaching and writing.

When she was thirty-three years old, the Shadd family—tired of the slow pace of racial reform in the States—headed for western Canada, and Mary began her historic career. This remarkable woman wore many hats: schoolteacher and principal in several schools, politician, campaigner for women's rights, recruiting officer in America's Civil War, first African American woman to study law at Howard University, author, practicing lawyer, mother, proselytizer for the cause of freedom, and editor of the *Provincial Freeman* (Windsor, Toronto, and Chatham, Canada).

The Shaw, Utendale, and Boyd Treks North

Few records exist of early black families in western Canada.[6] Although many were literate, they moved into areas that were remote, primitive,

"Wildwood" School, Junkins, Alberta, about 1923, home and school
to many black children in the early decades of the twentieth century.

(Courtesy of Morris and Yvonne Boyd, Edmonton, Alberta.)

and lacking systematized record keeping. Occasionally, however, both records and photographs survived. The Shaw and Boyd families of western
Canada provide rare case studies of outward migration from the United
States and Europe, as well as pioneering spirits that are remarkable for
their strength and endurance.

As with most early black Canadian families, the story begins several
generations ago, in this case with a woman named Lucretia, a Cherokee
who married Timothy Armstrong in Indian Territory (present-day Oklahoma). Although Lucretia never went to Canada, she was progenitor of a
family that would help settle three western Canadian provinces.

Standing more than six feet tall, Timothy Armstrong was a slave to the
Cherokees. The Indians praised him for his skill in hunting and in battle,
however, and eventually gave him his freedom.[7]

Lucretia and Timothy had two daughters. The younger, Lily, was
born in 1882. At sixteen, Lily married Walter Rolly Shaw, son of a furniture salesman.

Lucretia Armstrong
in Anadarko, Indian
Territory, about 1880.

(Courtesy of Kent Utendale,
Vancouver, British Columbia.)

Timothy Armstrong in
Anadarko, about 1880.

(Courtesy of Kent Utendale,
Vancouver, British Columbia.)

Lily Armstrong, 1898.
Standing barely four feet tall,
Lily married Walter Rolly
Shaw prior to moving to
Canada after the turn of
the twentieth century.

(Courtesy of Kent Utendale,
Vancouver, British Columbia.)

Walter Rolly Shaw's
wedding picture, 1898.

(Courtesy of Kent Utendale,
Vancouver, British Columbia)

Rufus Shaw is shown in front of his store in Anadarko, Oklahoma Territory, circa 1895. The sign above the door reads, "Rufus Shaw Furniture Bought and Sold."

(Courtesy of Kent Utendale, Vancouver, British Columbia.)

Interior of Shaw's store, about 1895.

Walter Rolly Shaw's sisters, Janie and Maggie Shaw, in Anadarko, circa 1890. Maggie (*seated*) was approximately twenty-five years old, and Janie was sixteen.

(Courtesy of Kent Utendale, Vancouver, British Columbia.)

Walter Shaw traveled the same roads taken by other young black men of his time. At his birth in 1880 in Nashville, Tennessee, his parents named him after Sir Walter Raleigh but misspelled his middle name. His father hailed from County Cork, Ireland; his mother was a black Tennessean.

Like many others, Walter searched for more promising possibilities in life. Unlike many others, however, this man who stood five foot three showed a determination to live and prosper.

Shortly after Walter and Lily married, they decided to look elsewhere for a place to live. The poor economic and social environment of Oklahoma drove the young couple to emigrate to Canada. In 1908, joining a large group of black men and women, they moved to Junkins (one hundred miles west of Edmonton). Two years later, Lily bore the first of her four children—Albert, Thomas, Ruth Mae, and James.

Lily and Walter soon branched out from their farming operation to run a grocery store to help support their children. All became pioneering Canadians on their own; their children and grandchildren live today in Alberta, British Columbia, and Saskatchewan.

Amber Valley, British Columbia. This verdant, rolling area lured
black homesteaders to western Canada from 1890 to the 1920s.

(Photo by the author, summer 1996.)

The Athabasca River flows through the town of Athabasca, Alberta.
Also a railhead and a landing on the river, the site was a jumping-off place for
immigrant Ukrainians, Russians, and African Americans.

(Photo by the author, summer 1996.)

Junkins (now Wildwood), in northern Alberta, west of Edmonton.
Shown is the family of Tony Paine, an early settler.

(Courtesy of Kent Utendale, Vancouver, British Columbia.)

Alfred and Susannah
Utendale, London, circa
1898. Alfred, whose parents
were Norwegian, married
a London woman prior
to moving to Canada.

(Courtesy of Kent Utendale,
Vancouver, British Columbia.)

Left to right: Iva Perrot, Barkley, and Sadie Miller, about 1900, before they moved to Alberta.

(Courtesy of Morris and Yvonne Boyd, Edmonton, Alberta.)

The mixed-race Kelly family, shown in Oklahoma, circa 1905, before migrating to Alberta.

(Courtesy of Morris and Yvonne Boyd, Edmonton, Alberta.)

The Kellys of Oklahoma, later of Alberta, Canada, were the children of Letha Boyd. More typical of immigrant families of the times, the Kellys reflected highly mixed racial and ethnic backgrounds. Joe Perrot married Iva Boyd, whose sister Ella had previously married George Kelly. Barkely Boyd's sister, "Aunt Atha," married a Chinese man, John Lee. Their son Wilbert married a Polish woman as his first bride and an English woman in a second marriage. This family represents just one example of mixed ethnic and racial married life on the Canadian plains at the turn of the twentieth century. For many, Canada did in fact prove to be a land of promises kept. ▢

14

Entertainers and Artists

BLACK ACCOMPLISHMENTS in popular entertainment have generated considerable controversy in our nation's history. While these diversions offered an escape from some aspects of racism, they often fettered black performers with subservience to (white) impresarios and business structures—whose main role seems to have been exploitation. Regardless, the freedom of education, travel, and income created by these opportunities offered new fields of occupation and expression denied to many minorities in earlier years.

In the mid-1800s black performers grew increasingly popular, especially in the West, where railroads allowed relatively cheap and easy transportation to audiences starved for diversion. Dancers, singers, comedy acts, touring theater groups, lecturers, Chautauqua presentations, religious tent shows, circuses, and more filled the idle hours of men and women weary of hard labor in isolated locations, and they served as community events for far-flung settlements.

MINSTREL SHOWS

To many modern observers, the minstrel show is a nearly forgotten artifact of post–Civil War American society. At that time, these comedy and music groups performed "snappy repartee" and were made up primarily of a few white men and a larger number of black performers.[1] Often outrageously racist, the skits offered exaggerated depictions of an illiterate black man ("Mister Bones") responding humorously to the white "straight man" ("Interlocutor").

In the first such performances, whites often played the black roles.[2] Later on, African Americans constituted most of the casts of these early touring comedy presentations. In the 1930s and 1940s African Americans disappeared from the shows, as the explicit racism of the format began to

Thomas "Blind Tom" Wiggins was a musician who toured American
stages during the mid-1800s. His original compositions were
unearthed in the late 1990s and are available in modern recordings.
His compositions numbered in the hundreds, and his active
repertoire included thousands of melodies. Born a slave, Wiggins
was "leased" by his master to a touring theatrical manager.

"J. C. O'Brien's Georgia Minstrels" pose on tour, circa 1890.

wear on even jaded audiences. The format lasted as a staple of American white fraternal and civic organizations well into the 1950s.

STAGE AND THEATER

Some believe American "touring theater" enjoyed its zenith in the last quarter of the nineteenth century. Large numbers of actors spread across America's more remote regions to bring Shakespeare, singing, and Terpsichore to mostly unsophisticated audiences hungry for a touch of "culture," or what could pass for it in those places. Culture, of course, implied musicianship, and, as with "Blind Tom," black performers drew attention, probably as much for their ability as for their rarity. Their proficiency in these performances began breaking down old stereotypes and brought African Americans more acceptance by white audiences, which in turn created greater choices in work and enjoyment.

This advertising placard, circa 1900, displays the "Wonders
and Thrills" that attracted audiences to a theatrical production
called *Across the Trail,* which included a black actor.

This image is from a Michigan family album, circa 1890.

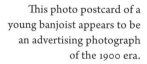

This photo postcard of a young banjoist appears to be an advertising photograph of the 1900 era.

Such risqué cabinet cards were popular
items of sale. What makes this one
doubly unusual is that "Corinne" is
of apparent mixed-blood heritage.

The "cakewalk" derived from an African American contest in
which slaves parodied strutting southern whites. In 1898, it was
adopted into a Broadway play, *Clarindy,* and became a national
dance fad. Bert Williams, arguably the most famous black stage
performer of his time, was the first to popularize the cakewalk
into a vaudeville act with his partner, George Williams.

The snapshot of Bill Pickett is attributed to a young Barry Goldwater, later a U.S. senator from Arizona. Pickett is shown wrestling and forcing the animal to its knees.

(Courtesy of the Barry Goldwater Collection, Arizona Historical Foundation, Tempe.)

THE WEST AND THE MOVIES

The American West exists primarily in our imaginations, the reality being far too rugged, inexplicable, violent, mean, and confusing to easily grasp.[3] For more than 150 years, popular writers—and photographers—have created a fantasy world to suit the demands of readers. Minorities, especially blacks, played roles that are important in the real West, but less important in the fantasy West of dime novels and, later, mainstream motion pictures.

There were black westerns, however, that attracted large audiences in the African American community, though these movies were rarely screened in white theaters.[4] Based on the popularity of white westerns, these extremely low-budget productions emulated those B movies down to the actions of heroes, heroines, and comic-relief sidekicks and the use of music. Often, the performers appeared in two-reel short subjects, such as *Rhythm Rodeo*, which could be inserted or withdrawn as needed in theaters catering to whites or blacks.

Rhythm Rodeo was just one of a succession of short
films targeted primarily to black audiences.

Located in Jacksonville, Florida, the Norman Film Manufacturing Company produced dozens of movies, both silent and sound, targeting black audiences.

Come on Cowboy starred Mantan Moreland (*center, with woman*) as a singing cowboy who was forced by circumstances into crime solving.

Comedy westerns outnumbered their "serious" counterparts. Man-tan Moreland—better known to white audiences as Charlie Chan's chauffeur—starred in several of these films in the late 1930s. Often called "Google-eyes" because of his affectation of bulging his eyes for comic effect, Moreland was a singer and dancer who migrated from Broadway to Hollywood in the early sound era. He usually played racially exaggerated roles, though he did appear in an all-black production of *Waiting for Godot* and near the end of his life in an episode of Bill Cosby's first sitcom.

BILL PICKETT

Bill Pickett deserves more attention than is generally granted. Born as one of thirteen children of an ex-slave father in 1870, this Texan experienced firsthand the end of the "cowboy kingdom" of life on the open range. He turned his upbringing into one of the most successful rodeo perfor-mances in American history—certainly the most popular show of its type ever starring a black performer.[5]

Pickett's brand of aggressive cowboying influenced several generations of rodeo performers as he appeared before what eventually amounted to millions of fans in the United States, Mexico, South America, and Eu-rope.[6] His widespread appearances came at the same time that amateur photography exploded in popularity. Virtually every private collection of western photographs in the country includes images captured by lo-cals who attended his rodeos. Despite his popularity in the United States, Canada, and Europe, Pickett was still denied lodging in New York City hotels when the 101 Ranch Wild West Show appeared at Madison Square Garden. He also entered the arena through a back door, because of racist restrictions.[7]

Thomas Edison used his new motion picture device to capture Pick-ett in one of his documentaries about the 101 Rodeo, and black motion picture producers sought the cowboy to add action to their scripts.[8] Un-fortunately, no complete edits of any of these films exist today. Publicity materials, however, abound in the form of movie stills, window posters, "one-sheet" posters, lobby cards, and advertising handouts.

Pickett bridged the gap between western rodeo and motion pictures; his appearances and films attracted large black and white audiences, even if whites were probably drawn more by curiosity than hero worship. Most representations of blacks in films continued the shuffling, servile charac-ters perfected by actors such as "Step N'Fetchit" (Lincoln Perry). Unlike

A flyer for the 101 Ranch and Wild West Show out of Ponco City, Oklahoma, in the early part of the twentieth century.

Pickett created bulldogging, a rodeo event in which he bit a bull's lip; other
cowboys would alter his technique to subdue animals with ropes instead.
This image, taken at Laramie, Wyoming, circa 1917, shows yet another African
American cowboy, Thornton "Thornt" Biggs, in the background.

One of the earliest photos of Bill Pickett, this publicity still,
dated 1925, shows the young cowboy (*extreme right*).

Jesse Stahl was yet another black rodeo performer who appeared throughout the
West near the turn of the twentieth century. His act, a combination of steer wrestling,
roping, and bucking-horse riding, drew admiring comparisons to Bill Pickett.

these performers, Pickett served as the prototype of a more realistic—if
nonetheless action-oriented—type of movie. Pickett died in 1932, a few
days after being kicked in the head by a horse. In 1971 he became the first
African American inducted into the National Cowboy Hall of Fame.

Oscar Micheaux

Bearing a French Huguenot surname from his slave predecessors, Oscar
Micheaux was born in Illinois in 1884. At age twenty he homesteaded
a five-hundred-acre farm near the Rosebud Sioux Reservation in South
Dakota—an unlikely beginning for a young man whose life would be filled
with adventure on the streets of Hollywood. His life straddled the hard-
ships of the Old West and the burgeoning literary and movie opportunities
of the twentieth century. Micheaux epitomized black entrepreneurship and
was willing to do whatever was necessary to succeed on his own terms.

Although he wrote little about his own upbringing, he left autobio-
graphical traces in his first three novels, *The Conquest* (1913), *The Forged*

Oscar Micheaux: author, door-to-door book salesman, movie producer, screenwriter, director, film editor, book editor, and distributor.

The main character, Jean Baptiste, and his love, Agnes, from the frontispiece of *The Homesteader.*

Note (1915), and *The Homesteader* (1917), in which protagonists played out a young black man's life in the West—in this case, rural South Dakota near the hamlets of Gregory and Winner. Micheaux self-published seven novels and sold copies door-to-door, starting near his South Dakota farm. He harbored visions of a literary career early in life, but it was only after seeing D. W. Griffith's spectacularly successful (and vitriolically racist) *Birth of a Nation* that he saw the potential of this new medium to contain his own long multiple-character narratives.

Noble Johnson, a founder of Lincoln Films, an all-black film production company in Chicago, contacted Micheaux with an offer to film his novel, *The Homesteader*. In a seminal decision, Micheaux rejected the offer and—in a stroke of youthful excess—decided to do it all himself. For the rest of his life, he wrote, directed, edited, and distributed his own movies. He cajoled the best "Negro actors" of the day to work in his films, producing twenty-two in all. Primarily detective stories set in modern cities, these movies contained visions of black life that were remarkably consistent with white middle-class plotting: strong heroes, beautiful women in distress, and so forth.

Micheaux targeted African American audiences craving images on the silver screen of persons who looked like them. He achieved nearly instantaneous success, albeit limited to larger northern black audiences and smaller southern theaters. Mainly white critics decried his amateurism and lack of moviemaking skills, yet his audiences devoured his product, making him a major writer and director in their eyes.

Micheaux earned posthumous awards from the Black Filmmakers Hall of Fame and the Directors Guild of America in 1989. In 1995 the *Chronicle of Higher Education* lauded him as the primary pioneer black director in American film. He was memorialized with a star on the Hollywood Walk of Fame in 1987.

HERB JEFFRIES

Herb Jeffries made the most successful black western movies—and the ones with the highest production values.[9] Born Herbert Jeffrey in Detroit in 1911, Jeffries was a jazz singer who performed in Chicago nightclubs. His light skin—his mother was Irish, and his father was of mixed ethnicity— and good looks made him popular with audiences. He later moved to Los Angeles and performed in clubs there. He also starred as a singing cowboy in four films based loosely on themes from cheap B movies made at so-called Poverty Row studios in Los Angeles.[10] These films featured

Herb Jeffries, a musical star and the only "black cowboy
movie hero" of significance in American films, appearing
here as his screen persona, Bob Blake. He starred in
four all-black-cast western movies of the 1940s.

William "Hopalong Cassidy" Boyd exemplified the American
western hero in his numerous film and television performances.

all-black casts and targeted African American audiences, especially children. Jeffries often said that he wanted black children to have cowboy heroes with whom they could identify as clearly as white children did with the bulk of western screen heroes.

❋ ❋ ❋

Although virtually none of the films mentioned still exists in complete form, and no western movie produced a major black actor in a recurring role, the legacy of these images still affects modern audiences, actors, and screenwriters. In small ways, all of these entertainers—from Blind Tom to Herb Jeffries—surmounted some of the inequities of racism and denied opportunity in order to encourage more realistic representations of African Americans in the media. ▣

❧ 15 ❧

Nonphotographic Imagery

ALTHOUGH THIS BOOK is devoted primarily to photographs of African Americans, blacks were also portrayed in other nonphotographic media. Unfortunately, stereoview cards, tintypes, daguerreotypes, cabinet cards, and other images sometimes reinforced racial stereotypes held by Victorian and post-Victorian viewers.

ADVERTISING

With the development of high-speed and high-quality chromolithography and rotogravure processes, advertising gained new formats.[1] The use of giveaways, handouts, brochures, mass mailings, posters, trinkets bearing brand names—in short, anything that could be printed in color—exploded in the late 1800s. Virtually no large business was without them, and hucksterism abounded. Not surprisingly, images of African Americans were often used to fuel the fires of commerce, East and West. Often, the representations were innocuous; sometimes they were simply sad reminders of the past.

African American children served as some of the most popular advertising icons, and images of children promoted food, cleaning, and household items. Advertisers presented them invariably as poor, ill-clothed, and almost giddy, apparently overjoyed with their lot in life. Perversely, the ads also showed them as well fed, healthy, and possessing attractive facial features—as if to say that "things are not all that bad." These black stereotypes equated dark skin with lack of cleanliness, and the images seem to suggest that the color black could be washed away with the proper application of washing techniques and products.

From the 1890s onward, advertisers displayed images of black men, women, and children as people who pretended to the status of the majority but who lacked schooling, social grace, and economic achievement. ▪

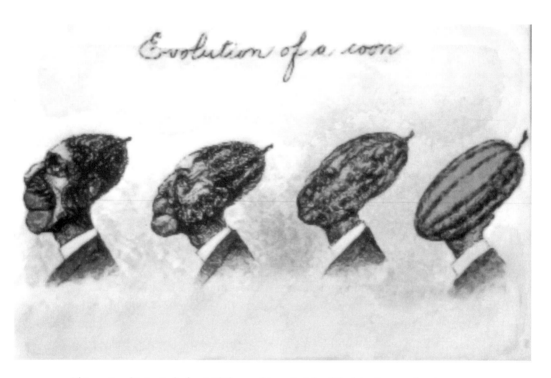

This postcard is typical of racist lithographic materials of the late 1800s and early 1900s.

A lithograph from the 1890 era focusing on the New York draft riots of 1862.

This lithographic stereoview card is typical of those found in living rooms during the late 1800s through the 1940s. It includes yet another artist's depiction of the Moor Estanevico ("Estevan"), who accompanied the Cabeza de Vaca expedition in 1540.

Images that portrayed happy slaves were popular well into the twentieth century.

This die-cut "nurse" was printed in Germany for sale in the United States.

"Collecting cards" such as this one are commonly found in Victorian-era scrapbooks.

CAMP LIFE IN THE WEST

This two page foldout in *Harper's Weekly* depicts roles of black army units in the West, complete with stereotypes of both blacks and Indians.

The Negro sentinel shooting the guerrilla Burroughs

Black soldiers are also found in these lithographs. It is emblematic that the enemy "guerrilla" is named, but the African American is not.

The title of this woodcut is "The Flag Is Come Back to
Tennessee." It represents the mythical "good" black servant
who has dedicated his life to the gentle southern man.

This entertainer performs before society women in this
not-too-fanciful rendering of the postbellum South.

These black entertainers with grotesque heads are typical
of the racist stereotyping of the day.

Little Pickaninnie, by Ida M. Chubb, continued the nearly relentless assault of racist imagery of the era.

"Wise's Axle Grease," an example of simplistic stereotyping of the times.

Afterword

AFRICAN AMERICANS still face many challenges. Prejudice continues to permeate the social and political systems of the twenty-first-century United States and Canada, though few would argue that it is as intense as it once was. However, only the most Pollyannaish among us would argue that mistreatment, distortion, and inequities have disappeared. Change is inevitable, and a changing view of the past is part of the present. As we collect more information about what has been withheld, misinterpreted, overlooked, or otherwise hidden from our view, we approach a more complete understanding of the issues. In that respect, this book began with references to historian Frederick Jackson Turner, who argued that the West is a unique product of the various social and ethnic groups who ventured beyond the Mississippi River. Europeans, Asians, Spanish and Mexican immigrants, African sons and daughters, and numerous other subgroups combined in the "development" of American society. With the exception of Native Americans, we are truly a nation of transplanted foreigners; it is the scope of this fact that makes us a modern nation unlike any other.

These pioneering men and women overcame barriers that most of us can only imagine; they contributed to a unique character called American. Exploring new lands is what humankind has done for all of its existence. The resultant infusion of energy, innovation, determination, and character not only carried black men and women westward but also helped give this nation its vitality.

Because this book focuses on my personal collection, put together over more than thirty years, it reflects both the span of black achievements as recorded in imagery and the predilections, peculiarities, and prejudices of their collector. It may thus reveal as much about the author as it does about the subject matter. In the case of these photographs, the mere fact that they were collected at all plus the obvious limitations of time and resources combine to constrain the content to not only what was important and illustrative but also what was available in the first place.

This heroic figure stood at the 1893 World's Columbian Exposition in
Chicago. Thirty years after emancipation, changes were slowly beginning to
take place in the depiction of African Americans in the larger society.

The Freed Slave, a statue created for the Columbian Exposition
in 1892, in St. Louis. Taken from *The Illustrated History of the
Great Exposition, 1892,* this is a nineteenth-century allegorical
image of a "new black man," set free from bondage.

    A personal collection is exactly that: items arbitrarily selected to suit the predispositions of the collector. It may include hidden agendas and ulterior motives, it may represent a broad and unbiased view of the material covered, or it may be so narrowly focused as to seem evangelistic; regardless, it is, at base, one person's reaction to the subject at hand. It is with all these motivations—and others unrecognized and unarticulated—that I have selected these three hundred or so images to represent a segment of American history that has often been overlooked.

    Pioneering black men and women, their families, and their solutions to the problems they encountered seldom make up the stuff of popular lore, even today when the mass media seem to pride themselves on their ecumenism. Modern writers often lump all things African American into a single poke, as my Missouri-born grandmother liked to say. The resulting jumble of oversimplifications comes from forcing too many divergent issues onto one subject; details are lost in the pursuit of larger issues. I am enamored with the details, especially those that can be shown in images

This tintype presents an enigmatic
image from the past that will always
remain subject to interpretation.

of mostly everyday individuals who sought to find productive lives for themselves and their children. They were, after all, taking part in a quintessentially American drama, played out on a stage that has essentially disappeared. Time leaves generalizations and stereotypes in its wake. Often, these simplifications become more "genuine" than the actuality itself. In this case, however, the images reproduced here left behind the undeniable evidence of the truth of these stories and persons.

Understanding the social milieu in which these images were created might help us achieve a deeper understanding of the individuals and groups represented. Old photographs are, generally, merely pictures of anonymous people; they are also vivid records of the achievements, longings, and values possessed by those people as they marched into American history. The fact that they were black is secondary, while the fact that their racial heritage was often dismissed is primary.

In sum, we can seldom know many of the truths silently contained in these photographs: who many of these people were will remain a mystery, where they lived we may only occasionally surmise, and the knowledge of how they spent their days, who they loved, or how they died is forever denied to us. We can make only educated guesses based on assumptions about photographers, styles of dress, tools and utensils, fashion, ornamentation, and the like. As these bits of paper, glass, and metal have changed hands for more than 150 years, too much has been lost for us to know definitely what coded messages these items were intended to convey.

What we do know is that this is as close as we will ever get to most of these people. What is left are the images alone, and they are often the sum total of what remains of these individuals and their passing. That knowledge, however, is rich in implication, if sparse in detail. The stories of African Americans are varied. In these likenesses we can see hundreds of individuals and groups who have left imprints through which they might gently strike the chords of our understanding. We see human beings in all their complexity; we see our common humanity.

Appendix

A *Short History of Photography*

Dating Old Images

THIS TEXT'S CENTRAL PREMISE is that imagery can tell us something about the past that words alone cannot. Whether images can compel attention more than words is the stuff of philosophical and literary confrontations, to be sure, but it is not the purview of this author to take on that debate. Instead, I have attempted to set imagery in the context of social history for the single purpose of illuminating if only a bit the shadowy nooks and crannies in history into which African Americans have often been placed. As a result, many readers will desire help in finding out more about their personal images—often of relatives and friends—whose identities and accomplishments have been forgotten, only to be preserved in fading photos. In order to help those who may wish to find out more about their imagery, this section has been added to help identify, date, locate, or further explain what they contain. Conclusively identifying imagery is often inexact, exasperating, and difficult, given the passage of time and changing social roles and assumptions, but it is worth the attempt. Besides, it can be great fun.

Within the past two hundred years or so since the first photographic process was devised, the medium has moved from shadowy smudges on paper to high-definition digital recordings—and at every stage someone has assumed that the processes could not get any better or more accurate. Despite that attitude, we find that much is always missing in the images that only newer technologies can seem to explain. Today we can enhance old photographs to the point that objects and details that were lost to casual viewing may be restored to view—all of which can alter the perception of the imagery itself. One can only wonder at what these same images will yield in another century.[1] That reason alone is enough to preserve and maintain these fleeting connections with our past.

With all that in mind, this section deals with the history of photography, especially as it applies to researchers who might need help in finding out more about their old images.

The Robert B. Pendleton family. This cabinet card was
discovered in an old trunk in Portland, Oregon.

"Mushing the Trail," in Alaska, circa 1880.

(Photo by P. S. Hunt. Courtesy of the U.S. Geological Survey Photographic Archives, Denver.)

MOST POPULAR FORMATS

Photography may be commonplace today, but nearly two hundred years ago it was "advanced science," carried out in laboratories and workshops by the leading researchers of the time. As a result, experimenters in Europe devised methods of recording light on treated paper, glass, carbon-coated sheets, potato slurries, sensitized cloth, ceramics, and other surfaces too varied to mention or whose exact formulas have been lost with the passage of time. Regardless, by the time the American frontier was being populated by westward-moving pioneers, photographers had already made reputations in the Civil War and Reconstruction. They, like most entrepreneurs of the era, followed the general exodus westward.

Though experimenters around the world had developed a variety of photographic techniques in the early 1800s, it was not until the middle of that century that preservation, stabilization, and duplication methods were developed, making photography safe, transportable, economical, and practical. Even in those days, however, the terms were relative: "safety" meant that highly caustic and explosive chemicals could be handled with reasonable assurance that the technician would not blow himself or herself to smithereens. Many did just that. "Economy" is always relative to need or desire; by the 1850s there were enough individuals, publications, and governments willing to pay the freight so that commercial photographers (a new occupational category) could make a living. "Practicality" meant that techniques for creating, transporting, and protecting glass negative plates and highly polished copper and silver surfaces could be accomplished in the field—thus requiring that horse-drawn, padded wagons be built to carry heavy, fragile equipment and scaled-down processing laboratories to the point where the images were to be made.

If photographic images are to be placed in proper historical and social perspective—and if one is determined to find actual or approximate dates for these photos—a rudimentary knowledge of the techniques and formats used to create them will be helpful to anyone interested in how we have come to possess and treasure these historical artifacts, who made them, when and where they originated, and how they might yield accurate and useful information.

Today, many argue that photography is the "father" of visual mass media. Magazine ads, photogravure printing, movies, television, videotapes, DVDs, and digital imagery are simply modern methods of preserving the basic concept of "light registered on a photo-sensitive surface" using the newest forms of duplication, storage, and distribution. Modern digital photography may not use sensitized silver halides to form images as in the days of pioneering photographers, but the content is analogous to those old grainy pictures made in earlier times.

Similarly, though a photograph made in 1860 might not be seen or distributed for months or years after it was recorded, today it often takes only microseconds to achieve the same result. The speed of the process has changed, but the content remains remarkably the same.

Provenance—verifying the source—of photographic images is often as difficult as it is in any work of art. Nearly everyone who looks at an old photograph questions its age, location, and methods of production. To that end, the following pages examine in a highly compressed manner how photography developed in Europe and the United States and how those events affected the images found in this book—and, quite possibly, the reader's private collection. Terms defined here may aid the reader in the search for clues about the sources and content of the photographs and lithographs displayed. In addition, knowing the process, location of the photographer, studio backgrounds, clothing, coiffures, and so on may help date and locate images that might defy easy detection.

The First Photographers

Jacques M. Daguerre began his working career in France as a stage designer and, like many early photographers, painter. During the 1820s his interests led him into an examination of how images might be recorded from life itself. He joined with Nicephore Niepce, whose scientific training included experimentation with the creation of faint images on metal plates. The result was the eponymously named daguerreotype, arguably the single most important development in the history of this new art and science of photography.[2] From this moment onward, realistic depictions of persons and places could be made in a stable, durable, economical, transportable manner.[3] As time would prove, the scientific potential was enormous; the economic potential was gargantuan.

Between the development of the daguerreotype in the early 1830s and George Eastman's Kodak (snapshot-making) box cameras in the late 1800s, a variety of similar techniques—some exotic, some simple—became widespread. A rising demand for "pictorials" of all kinds predated newspapers' introduction of photo reproduction: steel-pen drawings, lithographs, and freehand sketches filled the pages of *Leslie's Illustrated Newspaper* and *Harper's Weekly Journal of Civilization,* the two most popular publications of their times in the United States.[4]

Prior to the invention of cheap, mass-produced cameras that nearly anyone could buy and use, thousands of itinerant photographers began to hawk their wares in proliferation, plying the trade in large cities, small settlements, and railroad stops. Combining photographic skill, entrepreneurialism, and a keen sense of public desire for this newest-of-new technology, they produced millions of daguerreotypes, tintypes, ambrotypes, and glass plates. Resulting images were not simply developed and presented in raw form; they were often elaborately housed in leather, wood, mother-of-pearl, gutta-percha (an early form of resin "plastic") cases, silver bezels, golden-toned frames, and miniature lockets—to name only a

This daguerreotype was made circa 1855 by Augustus Washington, a son of slaves who was among the first practicing daguerreotypists in the United States. The man depicted is a black legislator who moved to Liberia during the Back-to-Africa movement of the mid-1800s.

(Courtesy of the Library of Congress, Washington, D.C.)

"Amateur Daguerreotypist," a lithograph from the 1890s.

few. Additionally, they were often tinted with lifelike colors that are impressive even today.

Photographers also created more unusual products that will be examined later. Clearly, the object of their passion was to make a living, but they inadvertently created highly attractive, enduring, and historically important evidence of social movements in a rapidly changing country.

By applying "painterly portraiture" to new and far less expensive media, these entrepreneurs-cum-artists not only satisfied their clients' desire for attention and authentication as individuals in a growing mass society but also—quite inadvertently—preserved part of American history.

DAGUERREOTYPES
(CIRCA 1830–1850s)

Daguerreotypes were thick copper plates that had been polished to a high luster and then single- or double-plated with sensitized silver. Somewhat uniquely, the exposures themselves were negatives, giving the illusion of positives when viewed with light reflecting off the silver coating underneath. The resulting images are amazingly lifelike, detailed, and possessed of an almost three-dimensional quality that is only apparent when seeing one in reality. Photographic duplicates of daguerreotypes lack a sense of depth and sharpness. Using "wet-plate" techniques, the photographer had to coat the plates immediately before exposing them and plunge them into the dangerous developing chemicals. They are difficult to replicate, even today. Because of the difficulty and danger involved, only the most highly trained professional could produce them. As a result, costs were high; an image might cost five dollars or more when the average daily wage was a dollar or less.

TINTYPES (FERROTYPE, MELAINOTYPE)
(1850s–1930s)

Tintypes were mid-nineteenth-century replacements for daguerreotypes, developed to meet the demand for cheaper processes that would be affordable to a larger public. To the general viewer, the relatively flat appearance of the image was more than offset by its lower costs and ease of production. Instead of a silver backing, tintypes employed an enameled sheet of thin, black iron that had been coated with a light-sensitive silver solution immediately before exposure.

This is an example of a tintype. Originally coated with cheap varnish
as a preservative, when found today they are usually darkened by
exposure to sunlight. Restoration is difficult and risky.

Inexpensive paper sleeves like this one
replaced booklike cases as photographs
found their ways into family albums.

Creating even more problems today, the images were coated with varnish or shellac to help preserve them. This technique means that most
tintypes found are darkened by time; the cloudy aspect is caused by oxi-
dation of the varnishes, not the image. However, only limited success has
been made to date in removing the coating. Therefore, like daguerreotypes, each image is an original. Copies, however, could be made by rephotographing the original, and business cards of many photographers
often touted the availability of such services. As with earlier processes,
keep in mind that these images are of reverses (negatives) of the subject.
What appears on the right, for example, was actually on the left.

These cheaper photographs were sold in exactly the same formats as
daguerreotypes: in cases, frames, tinted, and so forth. Since making tintypes was "dry" (not needing wet plates), much easier, and less hazardous than its predecessor, it was not long before tintype artists were selling
their wares in parlors, circuses, public halls, and train stations across the
country. The portability of the process enabled the profession of itinerant
photography to blossom and move westward.

An exotic woman, possibly from the West Indies.
This ambrotype was found in New York State.

Oddly for these early processes, tintypes can still be made today, and the materials are readily available from many retailers. Therefore, do not assume that any tintype found is "old"; it could be a modern re-creation.

AMBROTYPES (AMBRIOTYPES)
(CIRCA 1851–CIRCA 1890)

Invented by Frederick S. Archer, ambrotypes were produced by creating an underexposed negative on a glass plate. Somewhat resembling the daguerreotype, ambrotypes were mounted on a backing sheet; however, in this method the image was visible only when the glass plate was mounted on top of a black backing, usually paper or velvet. Whereas the daguerreotype was expensive to produce, the ambrotype was substantially lower in cost. However, both processes were hazardous for photographers.[5]

Ambrotypes and daguerreotypes competed head-to-head, but the ambrotypes' advantages of lower costs plus an image that could be viewed from any angle gave it an advantage. Daguerreotypes had to be tilted from side to side to yield the best result. For this and other reasons, the early format waned in popularity.

A glass-plate negative. When "prints" (copies) became possible by exposing sensitized paper to light that had passed through the negative, older forms of photography began to fade from popularity.

Since the large negatives contained much more visual information (number of silver halide particles), subsequent images could be enlarged and cropped as the customer required.

GLASS PLATES
(CIRCA 1840S–1940)

Glass-plate photographs were made with glass substituting for metal backing. The first "wet plate on glass" images were produced in France by Abel N. de Saint-Victor. By the late 1840s, this process—which used caustic silver nitrate—had become a popular medium for the production of art-grade images and government-backed projects.[6] Paper was also coated the same way to produce albumen prints, since egg whites were part of the chemistry. A safer and more manageable dry-plate process followed and is discussed below.

CYANOTYPES

The strange blue-tinted cyanotypes are today associated with blueprints used by architects and engineers. Derived from a mid-1800 invention by one of several contenders for the honor, they are the result of a search for a way to print images on paper or other lightweight media, since the metals and glass of the period were expensive and clumsy.

Albumen cabinet cards like this one, c. 1890, can produce excellent
images that last long and hold their "densities" (black-and-white contrast
ratios) well. However, as mass production put pressures on quality, the
photos produced by this means resulted in images that become thin
and brown-toned over the years, especially if exposed to sunlight.

This cyanotype is a rare outdoor image taken in Michigan, circa 1890.

The process involved the use of sunlight, various chemicals, and the production of Prussian blue, the agent by which the image itself was formed. They fade relatively quickly and are best stored in total darkness in an acid-free environment.

Stereopticons and "Stereoviews"
(1830s–1940s)

Creating the illusion of three dimensions in an image was apparently accomplished with toys in ancient Egypt, Greece, and Rome, judging from evidence found in archaeological explorations. In 1838 Sir Charles Wheatstone patented a device that used pairs of images that were photographed while slightly offset from each other to produce an illusion of depth with mirrors and prisms. In America, however, it was in 1862 that Oliver Wendell Holmes Sr. and his partner, Joseph Bates, introduced the Holmes Stereopticon; this device revolutionized the use of three-dimensional entertainment and can still be found in antique markets and masquerading as the modern Viewmaster in toy stores.

"Stereos" made by local photographers are rare, however, since large companies dominated their production, meeting demands for the millions

Keystone View Company and other smaller firms produced millions
of these dual-image cards. Mounted on stiff cardboard, they created the
illusion of three dimensions when viewed with a stereoscope.

of copies that were being snapped up at a prodigious rate. So popular were
these devices that they might be considered the "television" of Victorian
times. Libraries, schools, churches, and most middle-class parlors sported
collections of these images, stored in albums. There were twenty or more
major manufacturers of these images, and the photographers traversed
the world, searching out the arcane and unusual. Images of blacks were
common, invariably—and sadly—stereotyping them as servile, unedu-
cated, and poor. More than one generation of whites had their visions of
these men, women, and children tainted by the narrow views of African
American life.

Cartes de Visite (1854–1860s) and Cabinet Cards (1866–1910)

Among the most popular photographic formats, cabinet cards[7] and *cartes
de visite* allow both the collector and the student of history a large source
of information about the subjects and their locations, photographers, and
social environments in general. Produced in essentially the same manner,
both were albumen prints on stiff Bristol-board card stock.[8] (Before 1870,

Edward Middlefoot in a carte de visite from one of Ball and Thomas's Cincinnati studios. Often costing less than ten cents each, carte de visites were created by the millions and were truly the low-cost photograph of their times.

Photographs were subject to taxation during the Civil War, and many carte de visites and fewer cabinet cards will have a dated and canceled Internal Revenue stamp on the reverse.

Shown actual size, this small cabinet card shows how
amateur photographers were able to have their images
mounted on boards similar to professional standards.

this kind of board was made like single-layer "cardboard." After 1870, it appears more like pressed board.)

Tracing their genesis to Arthur Disderi, a photographer who developed a process to place multiple exposures on one negative, these small
(2 1/2 x 4 1/2 inches) images could be produced at far lower costs than tintypes and daguerreotypes. They were often called "calling cards" and were
presented when visiting. Disderi's development created savings in chemicals, sensitized plates, and time.

Cabinet cards rapidly replaced cartes de visite in the mid-1860s since they were larger, more affordable than life-size portraits, easy to transport and send by mail, and most importantly, the result of far better processing. Many cabinet card images found today are sharp, photographically detailed, and possess clarity and liveliness not found in many modern photographs.

For those interested in dating images, these two formats hold a variety of clues: The bottom margins and reverses are often printed with the names and locations of the photographers. Printers of card stock also changed their styles from year to year, and a comparison of cards from the same studio will often give a hint—not a precise date, necessarily—of the year of its making. Marginalia are often found on the reverses, giving even more information about the photography and its subject. Styles of ornamentation changed over the decades as well. With detective work, these can be compared and dated.[9]

Dating Chart

The following chart is largely derived from Ron and Maureen Willis's "Photography as a Tool in Genealogy."[10]

CARD COLORS

1866–1880	white card stock of light weight
1880–1890	different colors for face and back of mounts
1882–1888	face of bluff, matte-finished, back creamy yellow, glossy

BORDERS

1866–1880	red or gold rules, single and double lines
1883–1885	wide gold borders
1885–1892	gold beveled edges
1889–1896	rounded corner rule, single line
1890–1892	metallic green or gold-embossed border
1896	impressed outer border without color

CORNERS

1866–1880	square, lightweight mount
1880–1890	square, heavy Bristol-board with scalloped sides

This "turning leaf" style of cabinet card was usually reserved for images of deceased persons.

This image is a stylized sketch of supposed everyday black life mounted on a "boudoir" cabinet card. Entrepreneurial photographers were constantly searching for new, innovative formats that would appeal to their customers. As a result, collectors and researchers are still stumbling upon unusual sizes and shapes.

Another list of standard photographic image sizes may also be helpful in tracing formats and dates. It is important to note that most photographers cut their images to these sizes, beginning with daguerreotypes:

Full (whole) plate	6 1/2 x 8 1/2 inches
Half plate	4 1/4 x 6 1/2 inches
Quarter plate	3 1/4 x 4 1/4 inches
One-sixth plate	2 1/4 x 3 1/4 inches
One-eighth plate	2 1/8 x 3 1/4 inches
One-sixteenth plate	1 5/8 x 2 1/8 inches

Similarly, a listing of photographic mount sizes helps identify the origins of images:[11]

Carte de visite	4 1/4 x 2 1/2 inches
Cabinet card	4 1/2 x 6 1/2 inches
Victoria	5 x 3 1/4 inches
Promenade	7 x 4 inches
Boudoir	5 1/4 x 8 1/2 inches
Imperial	6 7/8 x 9 7/8 inches
Panel	4 x 8 1/4 inches
Stereograph	3 x 7 inches

Dry-Plate Photography and the Kodak Revolution (1880–)

The foregoing formats of image making dominated the latter half of the nineteenth century, but demand began to outstrip production capabilities of photographers, no matter what processes they used. George Eastman, a self-trained chemist and experimenter with little formal schooling, was addicted to photography. The wet-plate photographs he made were a constant irritation, so when he read about an English "dry-plate" development, he eagerly sought financial backing to bring the process to the United States.

This tiny card, shown actual size, illustrates the endless ingenuity of photographers in creating unusual products.

In brief, Eastman set up a business in which customers bought his dry glass plates in sealed packages—this new process no longer required wet chemicals. After loading them in darkness into the proprietary, of course, Eastman Cameras (of his own invention), they were exposed and then returned to the company for processing and printing, if desired. This development revolutionized photography, making it far easier and cheaper than before.

Furthering his business, in 1884 he patented "roll film" that eliminated glass plates entirely. Amateurs as well as professionals could purchase rolled strips of sensitized photographic film, place them in cameras, and produce as many images as they wished. The day of the snapshot arrived and heralded the death of the ubiquitous, itinerant professional photographer-at-large.

In 1888, Eastman's company designed and sold the legendary Kodak Brownie camera.[12] By 1900, more than 250,000 "No. 1 Brownies" were sold for less than five dollars each. Its low cost and ease of use essentially turned photography from a trade into a hobby throughout the world.

Real Photo Postcards
(1902–1950s)

Beginning in 1902, Kodak offered to return prints from the factory with "Post Card" printed on the reverses. These were amazingly popular, and millions of original photographs were made for the sole purpose of mailing to friends and loved ones, often with the vacuous "Having a wonderful time" or "Wish you were here" written on the mailing side or implanted boldly on the image itself, automatically giving researchers a wealth of provenance information. They were used as keepsakes, since the thicker paper was more durable than the snapshot's thin paper. One main side effect was that these pictures often remained in the possessions of families far longer than the cheaper, less durable prints.

Proving to be more popular than expected, personalized postcards became a social rage.[13] Though targeted at amateurs, they were adopted by professionals as well. Business firms adopted them because of their immediacy and attractiveness. Photographers saw them as another format to offer their customers. Rotogravure companies were created with the sole purpose of manufacturing and selling them to tourists as mementos.

This "real photo post card" is an example of a photo that was made into
a postcard. Pushed to one side, the image allowed room for notation on
the same side, per U.S. Post Office Department rules prior to 1907.

Many photographs were little more than spur-of-the-moment items. These casual
"snapshot" images usually indicate more about the persons being photographed
and their living conditions than do the professionally produced images.

Professionally made photographs are often found on postcards, too.
This one could have been made expressly for the card, or it might have
been copied from a cabinet card or another more expensive print.
Sometimes, the imprints of photo parlors will be included on the
card or will show up as a faint, ghostly image on the bottom edge.

This postcard was produced by the black southern photographer Arthur Bedou and was made to be sold as a souvenir. Beginning in the early 1900s, millions of these cards were made and sold; they are for sale today, just as they were one hundred years ago— and seem to be as popular with tourists and collectors as they ever were. The "AZO" trade name indicates that the postcard was manufactured between 1904 and 1918.

OTHER FORMATS

The variety of photographic images is exceedingly large, and no single volume such as this could do more than begin to examine any but the most popular and available formats. Trade cards, advertising cards, counter cards, magic-lantern slides, glass slides, collotypes, salt-prints, opaltypes, autochromes, tinted images[14] of all stripes, and more add to the enjoyment and sense of discovery for those who examine these images in detail. ▨

Notes

PREFACE

1. This number is generally accepted by scholars of the American West and is reported in Charles H. Wesley and Patricia Romero, *Negro Americans in the Civil War,* 17.

CHAPTER 1

1. James Beckworth's slave master was also his father.

CHAPTER 4

1. Women also owned studios, but mostly in the East. Few examples of the work of women from this time can be found, but more is coming to light. See Jeanne Moutoussamy-Ashe, *Viewfinders: Black Women Photographers.*

2. The author is indebted to author and historian Paul Stewart of Denver for information about John Green.

3. James Ball Jr. was also editor of a newspaper, the *Colored Citizen.*

4. Panoramic paintings were a common form of entertainment in this era. The large canvases were rolled like scrolls on vertical posts that, when turned, created a "moving" image that was often accompanied by narration and music.

5. The full title of the booklet was *Ball's Splendid Mammoth Pictorial View of the United States Comprising Views of the African Slave Trade of Northern and Southern Cities; of Cotton and Sugar Plantations; of the Mississippi, Ohio and Susquehanna Rivers, Niagara Falls, E&c.*

6. Ball was also a "colored" delegate to the Republican National Convention in 1894.

7. J. S. McNeilly, "Ku Klux Klan in Mississippi," 150.

8. Jeanne Moore of Honolulu has researched Alice A. Ball for more than a decade and is a font of knowledge about the younger Miss Ball.

9. The author in indebted to Suzy Keasler of the Marion–Lee County Museum in Missouri for her biographical materials about William Hines Furbush.

10. George Williams, *History of the Negro Race in America,* 141–43.

CHAPTER 5

1. John J. Pershing was given the nickname "Black Jack" after his assignments to the Tenth Cavalry in Arizona as a young man. Later, when he attended West Point, his fellow

cadets used the term in derision. At first, Pershing was irritated by the sobriquet. Later, however, he seemed to warm to the unofficial title and its inferences, becoming proud of the bravery and loyalty of the black troops he commanded on forays against Pancho Villa. He used the nickname for the rest of his life.

2. Fort D. A. Russell, now F. E. Warren Air Force Base, was the only military installation to house—at different times—all four black military divisions. At one time, three were in residence simultaneously.

3. Many commanders desired to form upwards of a dozen all-black units, with various designations in both infantry and cavalry. Ultimately, a much reduced number of units was decided upon by the War Department.

4. According to Mary Davis of the Fort Davis National Historical Site in Texas, the term was first used in a letter written in 1872 by Mary M. A. Row, the wife of a Third Cavalry lieutenant, writing from Camp Supply, Indian Territory: "The colored troops (called by the Comanches the `buffalo soldiers' because like the buffalo, they are wolly [*sic*]."

5. A series of legal pronouncements found in Mexican archives showed these runaways to be a constant source of irritation between proslavery forces in Texas and the Mexican government, which was reluctant to force their return. Only after emancipation did some begin to drift back into Texas.

6. Often referred to in texts as "Negro-Seminole Indian scouts," these men, whose headquarters was located near Uvalde, Texas, today prefer a designation that emphasizes their American Indian and military roots, freely acknowledging, however, that they are descendants of black soldiers who formed the first units.

CHAPTER 6

1. The term *cowboy* was not commonly used. *Cowpoke, cowhand,* and *brushpopper* (for young wranglers of livestock) were the terms preferred by the men doing the work. The number of men in the cowboying trade is difficult to assess; few records exist except in the largest cattle operations. What they indicate is a *minimal* number of forty thousand total employment, with 25 to 30 percent African Americans, Hispanics, and American Indians (Jordan n.d., 165).

2. In motion pictures of the 1930s and 1940s, especially, actor-singers Gene Autry and Roy Rogers were the most well known. However, it was Herb Jeffries, a black singer and producer of four western movies with all-black casts, who preserved the historical origins of those men of color who sang to cattle in order to quiet them.

CHAPTER 7

1. George Everett, "Mary Fields: Female Pioneer in Montana," n.p.

2. How a woman could become pregnant while locked in a territorial prison is a reasonable question. Unless she was pregnant prior to being imprisoned, the answer is obvious. Officials were eager to release their female charges as soon as possible. In fact, few women served full prison terms in the nineteenth and early twentieth centuries.

3. See Anne M. Butler, *Daughters of Joy, Sisters of Mercy: Prostitutes in the American West, 1865–90.*

4. The Aultman photographs are courtesy of the Colorado State Historical Society, Denver, which houses the collection. The collection includes about five thousand images—mostly glass plates, ranging over a period of nearly one hundred years—and is a priceless record of the West.

CHAPTER 8

1. Meriwether Lewis, *Original Journals of the Lewis and Clark Expedition, 1804–1806,* vol. 1, pt. 2, p. 185. York was Clark's "body servant," a term that signified the assignment of a young slave to his equally young master for companionship. Family records indicate that York, the son of slaves Rose and old York, was given to Clark by his father in 1799. The association lasted until Clark hired him out to another slaveholder, apparently because the friendship had ended. York was freed sometime after 1811 and, according to varying stories, either died in the South or—a more traditional western version—returned to the West, joined the Crow Indians, and died in honor sometime between 1815 and 1819 as a member of the tribe. The uncanny parallel to the story of James Beckworth's death still perplexes scholars.

2. Moor "Little Steven" (Estevan) was most likely the first black man seen by Indians in what became the American Southwest. Often referred to as the "discoverer of Texas," he was probably a runaway from a wrecked slave ship off the coast of Florida in the 1520s. As with many after him, he was aided in his escape by Seminole Indians who helped him find his way to Mexico. From there he joined Spanish expeditions into Indian lands, searching for the legendary Seven Cities of Cibola—the cities of gold—and may have been with Panfilo de Narvaez's search through Florida in 1528. Crossing what is now part of Arizona, Texas, and New Mexico, he was a member of several expeditions and was certainly an item of wonder—akin to York's reception—when he appeared on Indian horizons.

3. John M. Carroll, *The Black Military Experience in the American West,* 360.

CHAPTER 9

1. This section is based on the author's interviews with Bill Bailey in Edgemont, S.D.

2. Robert "Bob" Bailey was one of three brothers who served in various divisions of the buffalo soldiers around the turn of the twentieth century. The family tells of a wandering young Bill, who was always a concern to his father. It was reported that Robert was always searching for his son, Bill, a young man not prone to keeping regular work hours. The lament was so well-known to the family that Bill's niece Pearl Bailey based one of her most famous renditions on the Hughie Cannon song, "Won't You Come Home, Bill Bailey?" Cannon's song was actually based on the apocryphal wanderings of a black vaudevillian of the same name. Bill Bailey swore to the author that the earlier story is true.

3. Among the black women who worked as cooks and maids for the Custers, perhaps the best known is "Aunt Sally" Campbell, who is buried at Galena, S.D.

4. During the 1930s, Reeves achieved a degree of national fame in magazine articles and newspapers published on the East Coast. Also during this time, a young radio writer,

Fran Stryker, was searching for a character he could create who would appeal to listeners of popular radio programs. No known documentation exists to prove that Stryker used Reeves as his model for a lawman who worked in Texas and Oklahoma—a marshal who displayed great skill at storytelling, disguises, riding, roping, and shooting, and who wore a mask and also rode with an Indian companion. Could Bass Reeves be the prototype for the famous radio and TV character, the Lone Ranger?

5. See Arthur Burton, *Black Gun, Silver Star: The Life and Legend of Frontier Marshall Bass Reeves.*

6. The Chadron, Nebraska, photographs are reproduced courtesy of the R. W. Graves Collection, Chadron State University Library.

7. The following section could not have been completed without the help of Geraldine R. Stepp-Evans of Denver and Eleanor Stepp Johnson of LaBarge, Wyoming. The author is grateful for these friendships that have stretched over nearly thirty years. The story told is the result of interviews ranging over that time with Stepp family members, children and grandchildren of Alonzo and Esther Stepp. It also includes biographical materials supplied by Jane Lonice Stepp, daughter of William and Geraldine, and an unpublished autobiography by Geraldine Stepp-Evans of Denver. Additional acknowledgment must be made to Scotty D. Utz of Laramie, Wyoming, for his unpublished manuscript, "Stepp'N Up."

8. To further explode stereotypes about African Americans, Lon Stepp brought with him a small library. Among those books were John Abercrombie's *Inquiries Concerning the Intellectual Powers and the Investigation of Truth;* Charles Bancroft's *Footprints of Time: And a Complete Analysis of Our American System of Government;* Virgil's *Aeneid;* John Hart's *Manual of Composition and Rhetoric;* George Herbert's *Popular History of the Civil War;* and assorted hymn books, Bibles, mathematical texts, and economic theory works.

9. Stepp-Evans, 4.

10. Bill Stepp served on the board of directors of the association in the 1950s.

11. One small "gentleman's ranch" was in operation in 1998 near Cheyenne.

CHAPTER 10

1. Rudolph M. Lapp, *Blacks in Gold Rush California,* 13.

CHAPTER 11

1. Patricia Sackinger, "Research Project in Black History," 3.

2. In one of the minor ironies of our times, the U.S. Coast Guard named a cutter after Healy in 2000, and it remains in distinguished service to this day.

3. Along with Arabic names such as Ishmael (the narrator of the novel), Melville loaded his writing of *Moby Dick* with guarded references to black seamen. The name of the ship, *Pequod,* seems to be an indirect reference to the Pequot Mashantucket (black) Indians of New England.

4. This section is based on author interviews with Ernest Johnson in June 1995 in Cleveland, Ohio, four years before Johnson's death in 1999.

CHAPTER 12

1. The Polynesian term *haoli `ele `ele* translates as "foreign black," which was the closest native Hawaiians could come to describing the dark-skinned men and women who began to move to their islands in the early nineteenth century.

2. "Rolling alleys" were extremely popular in the mid-1800s, especially in Honolulu. Herman Melville, author and seaman, worked for a time as a pinsetter in one of them, but whether it was Allen's is not known (Robert C. Schmitt, "Some Firsts in Island Business and Government," 81).

3. Hawaii is the sole "royal kingdom" acquired by the United States, which makes its history beyond the experience of many mainlanders and difficult for them to assess. Various kings and queens of the islands hired black soldiers, sailors, household guards, and musicians. In 1812, for example, an African American surnamed Anderson was court armorer to King Kamehameha's nephew. Kenneth Wiggins Porter, *The Negro on the American Frontier*, 194.

4. Richard A. Greer, "Honolulu in 1838."

5. Jumping ship was not only common, it was also tacitly encouraged by ships' captains, especially on the return voyages when holds were crowded with cargo. Since the crews were not paid until they reached their home port, any missing sailor's bounty shares were retained by the captain or the ship's holding company.

6. As inventor of the toggle harpoon, Temple became part of whaling history with his iron killing lance with a T-shaped head designed not to pull free of the whale's body on retrieval of the massive carcass.

7. Albert S. Broussard, "Carlotta Stewart Lai, a Black Teacher in the Territory of Hawai'i," 129.

8. John A. Andrew III, "Betsy Stockton: Stranger in a Strange Land," 160. Many historians note that there were more blacks in northeastern states than in all the southern slave states and commonwealths.

CHAPTER 13

1. In southern Ontario, near the small town of Dresden, the Reverend Josiah Henson established a school for runaway slaves. An escaped slave himself, Henson formed a small colony in order to aid and educate the men and women who came to him. In his later years, he was befriended by a young Harriet Beecher Stowe, who apparently based not only the title character in her novel *Uncle Tom's Cabin* on Henson but also used his stories about slavery as the basis for much of the novel. The small compound is maintained today as a Canadian historic site.

2. *Maroon* is a term used to identify the descendant of black slaves who had escaped their Spanish masters prior to the British takeover of Jamaica. They were renowned as especially skilled fighters. The term—a corruption of *Cameroon*, the homeland of many slaves—has been both an epithet and a mark of distinction at various times in history.

3. William Francis Butler, *The Wild North Land*, 216–17.

4. David W. Leonard, *Delayed Frontier: The Peace River Country to 1909*, 140.

5. Frederick Jackson Turner, *The Frontier in American History*, 227.

6. The author is especially indebted to the following individuals for the material in this chapter: Dr. Kent Utendale of Langley, British Columbia; Maurice and Yvonne Boyd of Edmonton, Alberta; and Lemuel and Carol Lafayette-Boyd of Regina, Saskatchewan.

7. In March 2007, approximately 77 percent of the membership of the Cherokee Nation voted to strip those black runaways and their descendants of membership in the tribe.

CHAPTER 14

1. These mixed-race groups preceded the blackface minstrel shows that prospered from approximately 1900 to 1950 in American fraternal organizations, churches, schools, and civic groups. In these presentations, white men and women covered their faces with burnt cork and white lip liner while presenting comedy acts drawn from scripted booklets readily available from theatrical play companies across the country.

2. The term *jig,* which became a racial epithet, seems to have derived from Irish minstrel performers who danced an exaggerated Irish jig while in blackface makeup.

3. Readers may have to bear with the author, who spent nearly thirty years as a professor of motion picture history; he may well reflect an overemphasis on materials from the movies, especially as they relate to African Americans in the West.

4. "All-black cast" films were often referred to as "race films" by white producers and audiences. They were generally relegated to racially segregated theaters.

5. Colonel Bill Cody's West Show was the most popular of the genre, and he also employed former buffalo soldiers as part of his historical battle reenactment.

6. Cecil Johnson's *Guts: Legendary Black Rodeo Cowboy Bill Pickett* is the definitive text on this pioneer cowboy's life and accomplishments.

7. As detailed in Johnson's biography of Pickett, this was not unusual at the time.

8. More than one hundred African American moviemakers produced films for primarily black audiences in large northern cities and the rural South. Prominent among these were Astor Studios, the Lincoln Motion Picture Company, Colored Players Film Corporation, and the Norman Film Manufacturing Company.

9. "Herbert Jefferies," "Herb Jeffreys," and "Herb Jeffries" were variant spellings of this former big-band singer who appeared with Duke Ellington, Buddy Baker, and nearly every name band in the 1930s and 1940s.

10. These small studios (Monogram, Republic, National, and others) produced quick, inexpensive, mostly western films in three to five days to fit the demands of small theaters that could not afford the rental fees associated with "A" studio releases.

CHAPTER 15

1. These printing processes made large-scale production of full-color pictures both cheap and widely accessible. Manufacturers were among the first to seize the opportunity to present their wares in a new—and entertaining—manner.

APPENDIX

1. Long-term storage of photographic images is a major concern to archivists of all stripes as it becomes clear that there is presently no universal method of recording images for posterity. Digital storage is in its infancy and keeps changing with the rapidity of new technology. No one can be sure that the devices of the future will even be able to recognize the storage methods of the present.

2. In England, W. H. Fox-Talbot most likely produced permanent images on paper before these Frenchmen, but he did not publish his work until later. He was far ahead of his time, however, since silver halides-on-paper prints would be the overwhelming favorite of photographers for most of the twentieth century.

3. Daguerreotypes were deadly dangerous and cumbersome to produce. They required the use of hot mercury compounds, acids, and alkalis, manipulated by hand in small spaces (sometimes the backs of wagons). Exposures were long—often ten minutes or more—necessitating elaborate head braces and awkward poses for portraits. A short examination of surviving daguerreotypes betrays a host of chairs, stools, lecterns, and columns for the subjects to lean against during the long exposures. Smiling is seldom seen, for obvious reasons. Needless to say, many such images contain blurs caused by fatigue or movement by the person or animal being photographed.

4. *Canadian Illustrated News, Punch,* and England's *Puck* were commonly read throughout the eastern and coastal western United States. Both used large amounts of visual materials.

5. Virtually all early photo processes were dangerous, since they involved the use of ether, nitrated glycerin (later named "nitroglycerine"), caustic acids and "fixing solutions," shellacs, and varnishes. As with early motion pictures that used similar chemicals, fires and explosions were unfortunate side effects of the photography business.

6. As with many new technologies of the time, governments were among the first to support photography, even when costs were high. In the United States, federally financed expeditions into western territories usually included a photographer or two. Mathew Brady, William Henry Jackson, and Edwin S. Curtiss earned substantial incomes fulfilling government contracts. Were it not for federal backing, virtually no photographs of these times and places would exist today.

7. The source of the term is not universally agreed upon; however, this style of photography was intended to be displayed without a frame, probably to lower costs. In fact, large numbers exist with elaborate, engraved, gilded, and embossed "frames" press-printed around the image itself. Clearly, it was intended to be displayed by propping against a shelf in a cabinet or on a mantel.

8. As an interesting example of the interface of art, craft, and commerce, demand for eggs in Europe and the United States rose so dramatically that the supplies were often exhausted, calling for an increase in the production and popularity of this food source.

9. The Bibliography contains several standard reference works. See, for example, Family Chronicle, *Dating Old Photographs, 1840–1929;* O. Henry Mace, *A Collector's Guide*

to *Early Photographs;* Carl Mautz, *Biographies of Western Photographers;* Moutoussamy-Ashe, *Viewfinders;* and all of Deborah Willis's books.

10. Adapted from Ron and Maureen Willis's *Photography as a Tool in Genealogy.*

11. Ibid.

12. The "Brownie" was actually designed and manufactured by Frank Brownell, who claimed that the name was not eponymous. He claimed that it derived from the sobriquet of a mythical Scottish imp. Possibly, both derivations are true.

13. The U.S. Post Office did not ordinarily cancel the stamps on these cards with day and date. However, rough dating can be determined by the fact that prior to March 1, 1907, the Post Office ruled that only one side of the card could be used for the address; notation was allowed only on the image side. After this date, "divided back" cards were allowed.

14. Starting with daguerreotypes, hand tinting has been added to every type of image discussed. The skill with which early professionals added lifelike colors is often astonishing, rivaling present-day color film photographs. Advanced students of hand coloring can often date photos by the type and style of coloration.

Bibliography

Abramson, Joan. *Photographers of Old Hawaii.* Norfolk Island, Australia: Island Heritage, 1976.

Adams, John. *Old Square-Toes and His Family.* Victoria, B.C.: Horsdal and Schubart, 2001.

Addington, Wendell G. "Slave Insurrections in Texas." *Journal of Negro History* 35 (1950): 408–34.

Adler, Mortimer, ed. *The Negro in American History.* New York: Encyclopedia Britannica Educational Corporation,1969.

The Afro-American Texans. San Antonio: Institute for Texan Cultures, 1987.

Aldrich, Herbert L. *Arctic Alaska and Siberia, or Eight Months with the Arctic Whalemen.* Chicago and New York: Rand, McNally, 1889.

Ambrose, Stephen E. *Undaunted Courage.* New York: Simon and Schuster, 1996.

Amherstberg Regular Missionary Baptist Association. "A History of the Amherstberg Regular Missionary Baptist Association, Its Auxiliaries and Churches." Compiled from minutes taken by members. Amherstberg, Ontario, Canada, 1940.

Amos, Preston E. *Above and Beyond in the West: Black Medal of Honor Winners.* Falls Church, Va.: Pioneer America Society Press, 1974.

Andrew, John A., III. "Betsy Stockton: Stranger in a Strange Land." *Journal of Presbyterian History* (n.d.): 157–65.

Andrews, Clarence L. *The Pioneers and the Nuggets of Verse They Penned from the Graves of the Past.* Seattle: Luke Tinker, Commercial Printer, 1937.

Andrews, Ralph W. *Picture Gallery Pioneers, 1850–1875.* Seattle: Superior Publishing, 1964.

Aptheker, Herbert. *The Negro in the Civil War.* New York: International Publishers, 1938.

———. *To Be Free: Studies in American Negro History.* New York: International Publishers, 1948.

Athearn, Robert G. *In Search of Canaan: Black Migration to Kansas, 1879–1880.* Lawrence: Regents Press of Kansas, 1978.

Bailey, Linda C. *Fort Missoula's Military Cyclists: The Story of the 25th U.S. Infantry Bicycle Corps.* Missoula: Friends of the Historical Museum at Fort Missoula, 1997.

Baltich, Frances. *Search for Safety: The Founding of Stockton's Black Community.* Stockton, Calif.: F. Baltich, 1982.

Barbeau, Arthur E., and Florett Henri. *The Unknown Soldiers.* Philadelphia, Pa.: Temple University Press, 1974.

Barbosa, Steven. *Door of No Return: The Legend of Goree Island.* Dutton, N.Y.: Cobblehill Books, 1994.

Bardolph, Richard. *The Negro Vanguard.* New York: Rinehart, 1959.

Barnum, Francis. *Life on the Alaska Mission.* Baltimore: Woodstock College Press, 1893.

Barr, Alwyn. *Black Texans: A History of African Americans in Texas, 1528–1995.* Norman: University of Oklahoma Press, 1973.

Barrow, Charles Kelly, J. H. Segars, and R. B. Rosenburg. *Forgotten Confederates: An Anthology about Black Southerners.* Atlanta: Southern Heritage Press, 1995.

Barrow, Robert, and Leigh Hambly. *Billy: The Life and Photographs of William S. A. Beal.* Winnipeg: Vig. Corps Press, 1988.

Bearden, Jim, and Linda Jean Butler. *The Life and Times of Mary Shadd Cary.* Toronto: N. C. Press, 1977.

Beasley, Delilah L. *The Negro Trailblazers of California.* Los Angeles: Times Mirror Printing and Binding House, 1919.

Beckwourth, James P. *The Life and Adventures of James T. Beckwourth: Mountaineer, Scout, and Pioneer.* Edited by T. D. Bonner. New York: Harper and Brothers, 1856.

Beller, Jack. "Negro Slaves in Utah." *Utah Historical Quarterly* 2 (1929): 122–26.

Bennett, Herman Lee. *Africans in Colonial Mexico: Absolutism, Christianity, and Afro-Creole Consciousness, 1570–1640.* Bloomington: Indiana University Press, 2002.

Bentley, Leo W. *Canada and Its People of African Descent.* Pierrefonds, Canada: Bilongo Publishers, 1977.

Bergmann, Leola Nelson. *The Negro in Iowa.* Iowa City: State Historical Society of Iowa, 1969.

Bernson, Sara L., and Robert J. Eggers. "Black People in South Dakota History." *South Dakota History* 7 (Summer 1977): 241–70.

Bertley, Leo W. *Canada and Its People of African Descent.* Pierrefonds, Canada: Bilongo Publishers, 1977.

Betts, Robert B. *In Search of York.* Boulder: Colorado Associated University Press, 1985.

Beyer, Audrey White. *Dark Venture.* New York: Alfred A. Knopf, 1968.

"Black Hills Rancher." *Ebony* 9 (October 1954): 16–20.

Blasingame, Ike. *Dakota Cowboy: My Life in the Old Days.* New York: G. P. Putnam's Sons, 1958.

"Bloodline That Will Never Lose It's [*sic*] Power." Unpublished monograph of the Blakey/Blakely/White family, Yankton, S.D., 1985.

Bockstoce, John R. *Whales, Ice, and Men.* Seattle: University of Washington Press, 1986.

Bogden, Robert, and Todd Weseloh. *Real Photo Postcard Guide.* Nevada City, Calif.: Carl Mautz Publishing, 2006.

Bolster, William Jeffrey. *Black Jacks: African American Seamen in the Age of Sail.* Cambridge: Harvard University Press, 1997.

———. "To Feel Like a Man." *Journal of American History* 76 (March 1990): 173–99.

Bowser, Pearl, and Louise Spence. *Writing Himself into History: Oscar Micheaux, His Silent Films and His Audiences.* New Brunswick: Rutgers University Press, 2000.

Brawley, Benjamin. *A Short History of the American Negro.* 4th ed. New York: Macmillan, 1950.

Broussard, Albert S. "Carlotta Stewart Lai, a Black Teacher in the Territory of Hawai'i." *Hawai'ian Journal of History* 24 (1990): 129–53.

Brown, Robert O. *Collector's Guide to 19th Century U.S. Traveling Photographers.* Forest Grove, Ore.: Brown-Spath and Associates, 2002.

Buckland, Gail. *First Photographers People, Places, and Phenomena as Captured for the First Time by the Camera.* New York: Macmillan, 1980.

Buecker, Thomas. "Confrontation at Sturgis." *South Dakota History* 14 (Fall 1984): 238–61.

———. "The loth Cavalry at Ft. Robinson: Black Troops in the West, 1902–1907." *Military Images* 12 (May–June 1991): 6.

Bundy, Hallock C. *The Valdez–Fair Banks Trail.* Seattle: Alaska Publishing, 1910.

Burkett, Randall K. *Black Biography, 1790–1950.* Alexandria, Va.: Chadwick-Healy, 1991.

Burt, Olive W. *Negroes in the Early West.* New York: Julian Messner, 1969.

Burton, Arthur. *Black, Red, and Deadly: Black and Indian Gunfighters of the Indian Territories.* Eakin, Tex.: Eakin Press, 1991.

———. *Black Gun, Silver Star: The Life and Legend of Frontier Marshall Bass Reeves.* Lincoln: University of Nebraska Press, 2006.

Busch, Briton Cooper. *Whaling Will Never Do for Me.* Lexington: University Press of Kentucky, 1994.

Bustard, Bruce I. *Western Ways: Images of the American West.* Washington, D.C.: National Archives and Records Administration, 1993.

Butler, Anne M. *Daughters of Joy, Sisters of Mercy: Prostitutes in the American West, 1865–90.* Urbana: University of Illinois Press, 1985.

Butler, William Francis. *The Wild North Land.* London: Burns and Oates, 1915.

Calabretta, Fred. "The Picture of Antoine DeSant." *Log of Mystic Seaport* 44, no. 4 (1993): 93–95.

Canot, Theodore, and Brantz Mayer. *The Adventures of an African Slaver.* Edited by Malcolm Cowley. Garden City, N.Y.: Garden City Publishing, 1928.

Carlson, Paul H. *"Pecos Bill": A Military Biography of William H. Carlson.* College Station: Texas A&M University Press, 1989.

Carroll, John M. *The Black Military Experience in the American West.* New York: Liveright Publishing, 1971.

Carroll, Patrick James. *Blacks in Colonial Veracruz: Race, Ethnicity, and Regional Development.* Austin: University of Texas Press, 1991.

Carter, Kate B. *The Story of the Negro Pioneer.* Salt Lake City: Daughters of the Utah Pioneers, 1965.

Carter, Velma Thorne, and Wanda Leffler-Akill. *The Window of Our Memories.* St. Albert, Canada: BCR Society of Alberta, 1981.

Cashin, Herschel V. *Under Fire with the Tenth Cavalry.* London and New York: Tennyson, Neely, 1899.

Chambers, Melvett G. *The Black History Trivia Book.* Denver: Melvett Chambers, 1986.

Chase, Will H. *Pioneers of Alaska: Trailblazers of Bygone Days.* Kansas City, Mo.: Burton Publishing, 1951.

Chrisman, Harry E. *Lost Trails of the Cimarron.* Denver: Alan Swallow, 1961.

Chu, Daniel, and Bill Shaw. *Going Home to Nicodemus.* Morristown, N.J.: Silver Burdett Press, 1994.

Clayton, Lawrence. "Bill 'Tige' Avery." In *Cowboys Who Rode Proudly,* edited by James Evetts Haley. Midland, Tex.: Nita Stewart Haley Memorial Library, 1992.

Coates, Ken. *North to Alaska: 50 Tears on the World's Most Remarkable Highway.* Anchorage: University of Alaska Press, 1991.

Coe, George W. *Frontier Fighter: The Autobiography of George Coe, Who Fought and Rode with Billy the Kid, as Told to H. Hillary Harrison.* Albuquerque: University of New Mexico Press, 1938.

Coffman, Edward M. *The Old Army: A Portrait of the American Army in Peacetime, 1784– 1898.* New York: Oxford University Press, 1986.

Cohen, Stan. *The Trail of '42: A Pictorial History of the Alaska Highway.* Missoula: Pictorial Histories Publishing, 1992.

Coleman, Ronald G. "Blacks in Utah History: An Unknown Legacy." In *The Peoples of Utah,* edited by Helen Z. Papanikolas. Salt Lake City: Utah State Historical Society 1976.

———. "The Buffalo Soldiers: Guardians of the Uintah Frontier, 1886–1901." *Utah Historical Quarterly* 47, no. 4 (1979): 421–39.

Collings, Ellsworth, and Alma Miller England. *The 101 Ranch.* Norman: University of Oklahoma Press, 1938.

Connelly, Christopher P. *The Devil Learns to Vote.* New York: Covici, Friede, 1938.

Cook, Fred J. "The Slave Ship Rebellion." *American Heritage* 8 (February 1957): 60–106.

Cooper, Gary. "Stage Coach Mary." *Ebony* 8 (October 1959): 97–100.

Cox, Clinton. *Come All You Brave Soldiers: Blacks in the Revolutionary War.* New York: Scholastic University Press, 1999.

Crockett, Norman L. *The Black Towns.* Lawrence: Regents Press of Kansas, 1979.

Crouchett, Lawrence P., Lonnie G. Bunch III, and Martha Kendall Winnacker. *Visions toward Tomorrow: The History of the East Bay Afro-American Community, 1852–1977.* Oakland: Northern California Center for Afro-American History and Life, 1989.

Cruise of the Revenue Steamer Corwin in Alaska and the N.W. Arctic Ocean in 1881. Washington, D.C.: U.S. Government Printing Office, 1883.

Curl, Caroline, ed. *Edgemont: The River, the Rails, the Ranch Lands.* Edgemont, S. Dak.: Edgemont Herald Tribune, 1984.

Dalrymple, Priscilla Harris. *American Victorian Costume in Early Photographs.* New York: Dover Publications, 1991.

Daniels, Douglas Henry. *Pioneer Urbanites: A Social and Cultural History of Black San Francisco.* Berkeley and Los Angeles: University of California Press, 1991.

Davis, Lynn. *Na Pa'i Ki'i: The Photographers in the Hawaiian Islands, 1845–1900.* Honolulu: Bishop Museum Press, 1980.

Dayton, Edson Carr. *Dakota Days.* Hartford, Conn.: Edson Carr Dayton, 1937.

DeAngelis, Gina. *The Black Cowboys.* Philadelphia: Chelsea House Publishers, 1998.

DeGraaf, Lawrence B. "Recognition, Racism, and Reflections on the Writing of Western Black History." *Pacific Historical Review* 44 (February 1975): 22–51.

Dick, Everett. *The Sod-House Frontier, 1854–1890: A Social History of the Northern Plains from the Creation of Kansas and Nebraska to the Admission of the Dakotas.* New York: D. Appleton-Century, 1937.

Dixon, Thomas, Jr. *The Leopard's Spots: A Romance of the White Man's Burden, 1865–1900.* Garden City, N.Y.: Doubleday, 1903.

Dollarhide, William. "The Best Historic Photo Sites on the Internet." *Everton's Genealogical Helper* 61 (March–April 2007): 59–77.

Donaldson, Lilian C., and Robert E. Williams. *The Donaldson Odyssey: Footsteps to Freedom.* Seattle: Lilian C. Donaldson and Robert E. Williams, 1991.

Duncan, T. Bentley. *Atlantic Islands, Madeira, the Azores and the Cape Verdes in Seventeenth-Century Commerce and Navigation.* Chicago: University of Chicago Press, 1972.

Durham, Philip. "The Negro Cowboy." *Midwest Journal* 7 (1955): 298–301.

Durham, Philip, and Everett L. Jones. *The Negro Cowboys.* New York: Dodd, Mead, 1956.

Edwards, Malcolm. "The War of Complexional Distinction: Blacks in Gold Rush California and British Columbia." *California Historical Quarterly* 56 (Spring 1977): 34–45.

Ege, Robert. "Isaiah Dorman: Negro Casualty with Reno." *Montana Western History* 16 (January 1966): 35–40.

Emilio, Luis F. *History of the Fifty-fourth Regiment of the Massachusetts Volunteer Infantry, 1863–1865.* Boston: Boston Company, 1891.

Ernst, Robert. "Negro Concepts of Americanism." *Journal of Negro History* 39 (1954): 206–19.

Evans, John Thomas [James Williams]. *Life and Adventures of James Williams: A Fugitive Slave.* San Francisco: Women's Union Print, 1874.

Everett, George. "Mary Fields: Female Pioneer in Montana." *Wild West Magazine* (February 1996). Available online at http://www.historynet.com/mary-fields-female-pioneer-in-montana.htm/3.

Everette, Oliver Page. *God Has Been Northward Always.* Seattle: Bradley Printing and Lithograph, 1965.

Family Chronicle. *Dating Old Photographs, 1840–1929.* Toronto: Moorshead Magazines, n.d.

Farley, Emery Lynne. *Black Dance in the United States from 1619 to 1970.* Palo Alto, Calif.: n.p., n.d.

Farr, James Barker. *Black Odyssey: The Seafaring Traditions of Afro-Americans.* Ann Arbor: University Microfilms, 1989.

Faux, William. "Memorable Days in America." In *Early Western Travels, 1748–1846,* edited by Reuben Gold Thwaites, vol. 12. Cleveland, Ohio: Arthur H. Clark, 1826.

Fishwick, Marshall, ed. *The Black Soldier and Officer in the United States Army, 1891–1917.* Columbia: University of Missouri Press, 1974.

———, ed. *Remus, Rastus, and Revolution.* Bowling Green, Ohio: Bowling Green University Popular Press, 1971.

Fletcher, Marvin. "The Black Bicycle Corps." *Arizona and the West* 16 (Spring 1974): 219–32.

Flipper, Henry Ossian. *The Colored Cadet at West Point.* New York: Homer Lee and Company, 1878.

———. *Negro Frontiersman: The Western Memoirs of Henry O. Flipper.* Edited by Theodore D. Harris. El Paso: Texas Western College Press, 1963.

Folsom, Franklin. *The Life and Legend of George McJunkin.* Nashville: Thomas Nelson, 1973.

Foner, Jack D. *Blacks and the Military in American History.* New York: Fred Praeger, 1974.

Fowler, Arlen L. *The Black Infantry in the West, 1869–1891.* Westport, Conn.: Greenwood Publishing, 1971.

Fox, Stephen R. *The Guardian of Boston.* New York: Athenaeum, 1970.

Franklin, William E. "The Archy Case: The California Supreme Court Refuses to Free a Slave." *Pacific Historical Review* 32 (1963): 137–54.

Frazier, Franklin E. *The Negro Church in America.* New York: Schocken Books, 1963.

Frisch-Ripley, Karen. *Unlocking the Secrets in Old Photographs.* Salt Lake City: Ancestry, 1991.

Frost, Lawrence. *Custer's 7th Cavalry and the Campaign of 1873.* El Segundo, Calif.: Upton and Sons, 1986.

Gleaton, Tony. *Tony Gleaton: Tengo casi 500 anos [I Have Almost 500 Years: Africa's Legacy in Mexico, Central and South America.* Syracuse: Light Work, Robert B. Menschel Media Center, 2002.

Good, Kenneth G. *California's Black Pioneers.* Santa Barbara: McNall and Loftin, 1978.

Grafe, Willis R. *An Oregon Boy in the Yukon: A Story of the Alaska Highway.* Albany, Ore.: Chesnimus Press, 1991.

Graham, W. A. *The Custer Myth: A Sourcebook of Custeriana.* New York: Bonanza Books, 1963.

Greene, Robert E. *Black Defenders of America, 1775–1973.* Chicago: Johnson Publishing, 1974.

Greer, Richard A. "Honolulu in 1838." *Hawaiian Journal of History* 11 (1977): 3–26.

Gugliotta, Bobette. *Nolle Smith: Cowboy, Engineer, Statesman.* New York: Dodd, Mead, 1971.

Haley, James Evetts, ed. *Cowboys Who Rode Proudly.* Midland, Tex.: Nita Stewart Haley Memorial Library, 1992.

Hamilton, Kenneth M. *Black Towns and Profit.* Urbana: University of Illinois Press, 1991.

Hanes, Bailey C. *Bill Pickett.* Norman: University of Oklahoma Press, 1977.

Hardaway, Roger D. *A Narrative Bibliography of the African-American Frontier.* Lampeter, Dyfed, Wales: Edwin Mellen Press, 1995.

Harndorff, Richard G. *Lakota Recollections of the Custer Fight: New Sources of Indian-Military History.* Spokane: Arthur H. Clark, 1991.

Harrison, Edward S. *Nome and the Seward Peninsula: History, Description, Biographies, and Stories.* Seattle: Metropolitan Press, 1905.

Hausler, Donald. *Blacks in Oakland, 1852–1987.* Oakland: Donald Hausler, 1987.

Haydon, Henry E., ed. *Poems on Alaska, the Land of the Midnight Sun: By Authors Residing in the Territory.* Sitka: Alaska Press, 1891.

Hayes, Isaac Israel. *The Open Polar Sea: A Narrative of a Voyage of Discovery toward the North Pole in the Schooner "United States."* New York: Hurd and Houghton, 1874.

———. *Pictures of Arctic Travel.* New York: J. J. Little, 1881.

Henson, Josiah. *The Life of Josiah Henson, Formerly a Slave, Now an Inhabitant of Canada, as Narrated by Himself.* Boston: Arthur D. Phelps, 1849.

Higginson, Thomas Wentworth. *Army Life in a Black Regiment.* 1870. Reprint, East Lansing: Michigan State University Press, 1960.

Hodges, Graham Russell. *Slavery and Freedom in the Rural North.* Madison, Wis.: Madison House Publishers, 1997.

Holdredge, Helen. *Mammy Pleasant.* New York: G. P. Putnam's Sons, 1953.

Holmes, Edward, Jr. "A Brief Review of Black Cowboys in the Territory of Arizona." Ms. Arizona Historical Foundation, University of Arizona, Phoenix, 1984.

Holmes, Lewis. *The Arctic Whalemen.* Boston: Wentworth and Company, 1857.

Hottenroth, Fr. *Handbuch der Deutschen Tract [Handbook of German Dress].* Hanover: Curt R. Vincenz, 1979.

Hoy, Jim. "Black Cowboys." *Kansas* 18 (November 1986): 48–50.

Hunt, Frazier, and Robert Hunt. *"I Fought with Custer": The Story of Sergeant Windolph.* New York: Charles Scribner's Sons, 1947.

Innis, Benjamin. *Bloody Knife: Custer's Favorite Scout.* Fort Collins, Colo.: Old Army Press, 1973.

Jackson, Miles M. *And They Came: A Brief History and Annotated Bibliography of Blacks in Hawaii.* Durham, N.C.: Four-G Publishers, 2001.

Jacobs, Harriet A. *Incidents in the Life of a Slave Girl.* Edited by Jean Pagan Yellin. Cambridge: Harvard University Press, 1987.

Jeltz, Wyatt F. "The Relations of Negroes and Choctaws and Chickasaw Indians." *Journal of Negro History* 33 (1948): 24–37.

Johnson, Cecil. *Guts: Legendary Black Rodeo Cowboy Bill Pickett.* Fort Worth: Summit Group, 1994.

Johnson, Ernest, and Karl Kortum. "The Runaway and the Whale." *Naval History* (Spring 1991): 30–34.

Johnston, Hugh. *Canada's Ethnic Groups: The East Indians in Canada.* Booklet no. 5. Ottawa: Canadian Historical Association, 1984.

Johnston, Samuel P., ed. *Alaska Commercial Company, 1868–1940.* San Francisco: E. E. Wachter, Printer, 1940.

Jones, Howard. *Mutiny on the "Amistad."* New York: Oxford University Press, 1987.

Jordan, Bob. *Rodeo History and Legends.* Montrose, Colo.: Rodeo Stuff, n.d.

June, George H. *The History of Blacks in Canada: A Selectively Annotated Bibliography.* Westport, Conn.: Greenwood Press, 2003.

Kaplan, Sidney. *The Black Presence in the Era of the American Revolution, 1770–1800.* Washington, D.C.: Smithsonian Institution Press, 1973.

Katz, William L. *The Black West.* Garden City, N.Y.: Doubleday, 1971.

———. *Black Women of the Old West.* New York: Atheneum Books for Young Readers, 1995.

———. *Eyewitness: The Negro in American History.* New York: Pitman Publishing, 1969.

Kelbaugh, J. *Introduction to African American Photographs.* Gettysburg, Pa.: Thomas Publications, 2005.

Kelen, Leslie G., and Sandra Fuller, eds. *The Other Utahns.* Salt Lake City: University of Utah Press, 1988.

Kesey, Ken. *Last Go Round.* New York: Viking Books, 1994.

Langellier, John P. *Men a-Marching: The African American Soldier in the West, 1866–1896.* Springfield, Pa.: Steven Wright Publishing, 1995.

Langellier, John P., and Alan Osur. *Chaplain Allen Allensworth and the 24th Infantry, 1886–1906.* Tucson: Tucson Corral of the Westerners, 1980.

Lapp, Rudolph M. *Blacks in Gold Rush California.* 1966. Reprint, New Haven, Conn.: Yale University Press, 1977.

———. "Negro Rights Activities in Gold Rush California." *California Historical Society Quarterly* 45, no. 1 (1977): 3–20.

Larson, T. A. *History of Wyoming.* Lincoln: University of Nebraska Press, 1984.

Lasartemay, Eugene Pascal. "Jennie Daphne Prentiss: The Surrogate Mother of Jack London." Ms. Northern California Center for Afro-American History and Life, Oakland, n.d.

Lautenschlager, Virginia. "Mary, the Custer Family Cook." Ms. Hot Springs, S. Dak., n.d.

Leckie, William A. *The Buffalo Soldiers: A Narrative of the Negro Cavalry in the West.* Norman: University of Oklahoma Press, 1967.

Leonard, David W. *Delayed Frontier: The Peace River Country to 1909.* Calgary: Detselig Enterprises, 1995.

Leonard, David W., and Victoria L. Lemieux. *The Lure of the Peace River Country.* Calgary: Detselig Enterprises, 1992.

Lewis, Meriwether. *History of the Expedition under the Command of Lewis and Clark to the Sources of the Missouri River.* 7 vols. New York: Francis P. Harper, 1893.

———. *Original Journals of the Lewis and Clark Expedition, 1804–1806.* New York: Dodd, Mead, 1904.

Libby, O. G., ed. *The Ankara Narrative of the Campaign against the Hostile Dakotas, June 1876.* New York: Solomon Lewis, 1973.

Limerick, Patricia Nelson, Clyde A. Milner II, and Charles E. Rawkins. *Trails: Toward a New Western History.* Lawrence: University Press of Kansas, 1991.

Lobban, Richard A., Jr. *Cape Verde: Crioulo Colony to Independent Nation.* Boulder, Colo.: Westview Press, 1995.

Logan, Rayford W., and Michael R. Winston, eds. *Dictionary of American Negro Biography.* New York: W. W. Norton, 1982.

Long, Richard A. *Black Americana.* Secaucus, N.J.: Chartwell Books, 1985.

Love, Nat. *The Life and Adventures of Nat Love, Better Known in the Cattle Country as "Deadwood Dick," by Himself.* Los Angeles: Wayside Press, 1907.

Mace, O. Henry. *A Collector's Guide to Early Photographs.* Radnor, Penn.: Wallace-Homestead Book, 1990.

Malloy, Mary. *"From Boston Harbor We Set Sail!": A Curriculum Unit on African-American Mariners and Maritime Communities in Massachusetts.* Sharon, Mass.: Kendall Whaling Museum, 1993.

Mangan, Terry Wm. *Colorado on Glass.* Denver: Sundance, 1975.

Manion, Mae. *"Prairie Pioneers" of Box Butte County.* Alliance, Neb.: Iron Man Industries, 1970.

Maraniss, David. "Buffalo Soldiers." *Washington Post,* January 20, 1991.

Markham, Sir Albert Hastings. *A Whaling Cruise to Baffin's Bay and the Gulf of Boothia.* London: S. Low, Marston, Low and Searle, 1875.

Markle, Donald E. *Spies and Spymasters of the Civil War.* New York: Barnes and Noble, 1994.

Massey, Sara R. *Black Cowboys of Texas.* College Station: Texas A&M University Press, 2000.

Maur, Geoffrey. "Blacks of Phoenix, 1890–1930." Ms. Arizona Historical Foundation, University of Arizona, Phoenix, n.d.

Mautz, Carl. *Biographies of Western Photographers.* Nevada City, Calif.: Carl Mautz Publishing, 1997.

McCandless, Barbara. *Equal before the Lens: Jno. Trlica's Photographs of Granger, Texas.* College Station: Texas A&M University Press, 1992.

McLagan, Elizabeth. *A Peculiar Paradise.* The Oregon Black History Project. Portland, Ore.: Georgian Press, 1980.

McNeilly, J. S. "Ku Klux Klan in Mississippi." *Publications of the Mississippi Historical Society* 9 (1906): 150.

Micheaux, Oscar. *The Conquest: The Story of a Negro Pioneer.* Lincoln, Neb.: Woodruff, 1913.

———. *The Forged Note: A Romance of the Darker Races.* Lincoln, Neb.: Western Book Supply, 1915.

———. *The Homesteader.* College Park, Md.: McGrath Publishing, 1917.

———. *The Wind from Nowhere.* New York: Book Supply, 1941.

Middleton, Stephen. *The Black Laws in the Old Northwest.* Westport, Conn.: Greenwood Press, 1993.

Miles, Tiya, and Sharon P. Holland, eds. *Crossing Waters, Crossing Worlds: The African Diaspora in Indian Country.* Durham, N.C.: Duke University Press, 2006.

Miller, Edward A. *Gullah Statesmen: Robert Smalls from Slavery to Congress, 1839–1915.* Columbia: University of South Carolina Press, 1995.

Montana Historical Society. *F. Jay Haynes Photographer.* n.p: Montana Historical Society, 1981.

Montesano, Phil. "A Black Pioneer's Trip to California." *Pacific Historian* 13 (Winter 1969): 58–62.

Morris, Ann, and Henrietta Ambrose. *North Webster: A Photographic History of a Black Community.* Bloomington: Indiana University Press, 1993.

Moutoussamy-Ashe, Jeanne. *Viewfinders: Black Women Photographers.* New York: Dodd, Mead, 1986.

Mulroy, Kevin. *Freedom on the Border: The Seminole Maroons in Florida, the Indian Territory, Coahila, and Texas.* Lubbock: Texas Tech University Press, 1993.

Mumford, Esther Hall. *Seattle's Black Victorians, 1852–1901.* Seattle: Ananse Press, 1981.

Muraskin, William A. *Middle-Class Blacks in a White Society: Prince Hall Freemasonry in America.* Berkeley and Los Angeles: University of California Press, 1957.

Murphy, Robert Cushman. *Logbook for Grace Whaling Brig Daisy, 1912–1913.* London: Robert Hale, 1948.

Museum of Modern Art. *The Hampton Album.* New York: Museum of Modern Art, 1966.

Nankivell, John H. *Buffalo Soldier Regiment History of the 25th United States Infantry, 1869–1926.* Lincoln: University of Nebraska Press, 2001.

The Negroes of Nebraska. WPA Project. Lincoln: Woodruff Printing, 1940.

Newgard, Thomas, and William Sherman. *Plain Folks: North Dakota Ethnic History.* Fargo: North Dakota State University Press, n.d.

Newgard, Thomas, William Sherman, and John Guerrero. *African Americans in North Dakota.* Bismarck, N.D.: University of Mary Press, 1994.

Newman, Debra L., comp. *Black History: A Guide to Civilian Records in the National Archives.* Washington, D.C.: National Archives Trust Fund Board, 1984.

Nordyke, Eleanor C. "Blacks in Hawai'i: A Demographic and Historical Perspective." *Hawai'ian Journal of History* 22 (1988): 241–55.

Ogden, George Washington. "Letters from the West, 1821." In *Early Western Travels, 1748–1846,* edited by Ruben Gold Thwaites, vol. 19. Cleveland, Ohio: Arthur H. Clark, 1905.

Olcione, Amos, and Thomas Senter, eds. *Kenneth Wiggins Porter's "The Black Seminoles: A History of a Freedom-Seeking People."* Gainesville: University Press of Florida, 1996.

Oliver, Mamie O. *Idaho Ebony: The Afro-American Present in Idaho State History.* Boise: Idaho Centennial Foundation, 1990.

Organ, Claude H., ed. *A Century of Black Surgeons.* Norman, Okla.: Transcript Press, 1987.

Overstreet, Everett Louis. *Black on a Background of White: A Chronicle of Afro-Americans' Involvement in America's Last Frontier, Alaska.* Anchorage: Alaska Black Caucus, 1990.

Painter, Nell Irvin. *Exodusters: Black Migration to Kansas after Reconstruction.* New York: Alfred A. Knopf, 1977.

Palmer, Howard, and Tamara Palmer. *Peoples of Alberta.* Saskatoon, Canada: Western Producer Prairie Books, 1985.

Palmquist, Peter E., and Thomas R. Kailbourn. *Pioneer Photographers from the Mississippi to the Continental Divide: A Biographical Dictionary, 1839–1865.* Palo Alto, Calif.: Stanford University Press, 2000.

————. *Pioneer Photographers of the Far West: A Biographical Dictionary, 1840–1865.* Stanford: Stanford University Press, 2005.

Papanikolas, Helen Z., ed. *The Peoples of Utah.* Salt Lake City: Utah State Historical Society, 1981.

Pengra, Lilah Morton. *Corporals Cook and Cowboys: African Americans in the Black Hills.* Buffalo Gap, S. Dak.: Lilah Morton Pengra, 2006.

Petrov, Ivan. *Report on the Population, Industries, and Resources of Alaska.* Washington, D.C.: U.S. Government Printing Office, 1884.

Place, Marian T. *Rifles and War Bonnets: Negro Cavalry of the West.* New York: Ives Washburn, 1968.

Ploski, Harry A., and James Williams, eds. *The Negro Almanac: A Reference Work on the African American.* Detroit: Gale Research, 1989.

Polz, Ruth. *Black Heroes of the Wild West.* Seattle: Open Hand Publishing, 1990.

Porter, Kenneth Wiggins. *The Negro on the American Frontier.* Edited by John W. "Jack" Ravage. Stratford, N.H.: Ayer Publishers, 1996.

Powell, Anthony L. *The Buffalo Soldier on the American Frontier.* San Jose, Calif.: Portraits in Black, 1994.

Prather, Patricia Smith, and Jane Clements Monday. *From Slave to Statesman: The Legacy of Joshua Houston, Servant to Sam Houston.* Denton: University of North Texas Press, 1993.

Putney, Martha S. *Black Sailors: Afro-American Merchant Seamen and Whalemen Prior to the Civil War.* New York: Greenwood Press, 1987.

Ravage, John W. *Black Pioneers: Images of the Black Experience on the North American Frontier.* Salt Lake City: University of Utah Press, 1992.

———. "Blacks in the American West." *History of Photography* 16 (Winter 1992): 392–96.

Reflections in Black: A History of Black Photographers, 1840 to the Present. Washington, D.C.: Smithsonian Anacostia Museum and Center for African American History and Culture, n.d.

Remington, Frederic. *Frederic Remington's Own West.* Edited by Harold McCracken. New York: Dial Press, 1960.

Rhode Island Black Heritage Society. *Creative Survival: The Providence Black Community in the 19th Century.* Providence: Rhode Island Black Heritage Society, n.d.

Richards, Larry. *African American Films through 1959: A Comprehensive Illustrated Filmography.* Jefferson, N.C.: McFarland and Company, 1998.

Richardson, Marilyn. *Maria W. Stewart: America's First Black Woman Political Writer.* Bloomington: Indiana University Press, 1987.

Riley, Franklin L., ed. *Publications of the Mississippi Historical Society.* Vol. 9. Oxford: Mississippi Historical Society, 1906.

Robbins, A. C. *Legacy to Buxton.* Chatham, Canada: Ideal Printing, 1883.

Robinson, Charles M., III. "The Whirlwind and His Scouts." *Old West* 2, no. 8 (Summer 1991): 28–37.

Robinson, Gwendolyn, and John W. Robinson. *Seek the Truth.* Chatham, Canada: Gwendolyn Robinson and John W. Robinson, 1989.

Roosevelt, Theodore. *The Rough Riders.* New York: Charles Scribner's Sons, 1899.

Roper, Stephanie Abbot. "From Military Forts to 'Nigger Towns': African Americans in North Dakota, 1890–1940." *Heritage of the Great Plains* 27, no. 1 (1994): 127–53.

Rusco, Elmer R. *Good Times Coming? Black Nevadans in the Nineteenth Century.* Westport, Conn.: Greenwood Press, 1975.

Sackinger, Patricia. "Research Project in Black History." Ms. Archives and Manuscript Collection, University of Alaska at Fairbanks, 1974.

Sammons, Vivian Ovelton. *Blacks in Science and Medicine.* New York: Hemisphere Publishing, 1990.

Sandweiss, Martha. *Photography in Nineteenth-Century America.* New York: Harry Abrams, 1991.

Savage, W. Sherman. *Blacks in the West.* Westport, Conn.: Greenwood Press, 1976.

———. *On the Trail of the Buffalo Soldier: Biographies of African-American Soldiers, 1868–1918.* Wilmington, Del.: Scholarly Resources, 1994.

———. "The Negro in the Western Movement." *Journal of Negro History* 25 (1940): 531–39.

———. "The Negro on the Mining Frontier." *Journal of Negro History* 30 (1945): 30–46.

———. "The Role of Negro Soldiers in Protecting the Indian Territory from Intruders." *Journal of Negro History* 3 (1951): 25–34.

Schissel, Lillian. *Black Frontiers: A History of African American Heroes in the Old West.* New York: Simon and Schuster Books for Young Readers, 1995.

Schmitt, Robert C. "Some Firsts in Island Business and Government." *Hawai'ian Journal of History* 14 (1980): 80–97.

Schubert, Frank N. "The Black Regular Army Regiments in Wyoming, 1885–1912." Master's thesis, University of Wyoming, 1970.

———. *Buffalo Soldiers, Braves, and the Brass.* Shippensburg, Pa.: White Mane Publishing, 1993.

———. *Fort Robinson, Nebraska: The History of a Military Community, 1874–1916.* Ann Arbor: University Microfilms International, 1977.

———. "The Fort Robinson YMCA." *Nebraska History* 55 (Summer 1974): 165–79.

———. "The Violent World of Emanuel Stance." *Nebraska History* 55 (Summer 1974): 203–19.

Scoresby, Captain. *The Arctic Regions and the Northern Whale-Fishery.* London: Religious Tract Society, 1820.

Shaw, James C. *North from Texas: Incidents in the Early Life of a Range Cowman in Texas, Dakota, and Wyoming, 1852–1880.* Evanston, Ill.: Branding Iron Press, 1952.

Shepard, R. Bruce. "Plain Racism: The Reaction against Oklahoma Black Immigration to the Canadian Plains." *Prairie Forum* 10 (Autumn 1985): 114–21.

Shirley, Glenn. *Heck Thomas, Frontier Marshall: The Story of a Real Gun-fighter.* New York: Chilton Book Division, 1962.

———. *Law West of Fort Smith.* New York: Henry Holt, 1957.

Shreve, Dorothy Shadd. *The AfriCanadian Church: A Stabilizer.* Jordan Station, Canada: Paidea Press, 1983.

Siebert, Wilbur Henry. The *Underground Railroad from Slavery to Freedom.* New York: Macmillan, 1898.

Simpson, MacKinnon, and Robert B. Goodman. *Whale Song: The Story of Hawai'i and the Whales.* Honolulu: Beyond Words Publishing, 1986.

Siringo, Charles. *Riata and Spurs.* Boston: Houghton, Mifflin, 1927.

Smith, Gloria. *Black Americana in Arizona.* Tucson: Gloria L. Smith, 1977.

Smith, Herndon, ed. *Centralia: The First Fifty Years, 1845–1900.* Rochester, Wash.: Gorham Printing, 1942.

Smith, Jessie Carney, ed. *Notable Black American Women.* Detroit: Gale Research, 1991.

Spangenberg, Kristin L. *Photographic Treasures from the Cincinnati Art Museum.* Cincinnati: Cincinnati Art Museum, 1989.

Speidel, William C. *Sons of the Profits; or, There's No Business Like Grow Business: The Seattle Story, 1851–1901.* Seattle: Seattle Guide, 1967.

Stampp, Kenneth Milton. *The Peculiar Institution: Slavery in the Ante-bellum South.* New York: Alfred A. Knopf, 1956.

Stark, Sylvia. *Sylvia Stark: A Pioneer.* Seattle: Open Hand Publishing, 1993.

Stepp-Evans, Geraldine. "Alonzo Stepp." Unpublished ms., Denver, n.d.

Steward, Theophilus Gould. *The Colored Regulars in the United States Army.* Philadelphia: AME Book Concern, 1904.

Stewart, Paul W. *Westward Soul.* Denver: Black American West Foundation, 1976.

Stewart, Paul W., and Wallace Young Ponce. *Black Cowboys.* Denver: Black American West Museum and Heritage Center, 1986.

Stokes, Frederick. *A Negro Explorer at the North Pole.* New York: n.p, 1912.

Stover, Earl F. "Chaplain Henry V. Plummer: His Ministry and His Court Martial." *Nebraska History* 56 (Spring 1971): 20–50.

Struhsaker, Virginia L. "Doc Shadd." *Saskatchewan History* 30 (Spring 1977) 42–46.

———. "Stockton's Black Pioneers." *Pacific Historian* 19 (Winter 1975): 347–54.

Talmadge, Marian, and Iris Gilmore. *Barney Ford, Black Baron.* New York: Dodd, Mead, 1973.

Taylor, Quintard. *In Search of the Racial Frontier.* New York: W. W. Norton, 1998.

Thompson, Stith, ed. *Round the Levee.* Austin: Texas Folk-Lore Society, 1935.

Thomson, Colin A. *Blacks in Deep Snow: Black Pioneers in Canada.* Don Mills, Canada: J. M. Dent and Sons, 1979.

Thum, Marcella. *Hippocrene USA Guide to Black America.* New York: Hippocrene Books, 1992.

Thurman, A. Odell. "The Negro in California before 1890." *Pacific Historian* 19 (Winter 1975): 321–46.

Thurman, Sue Bailey. *Pioneers of Negro Origin in California.* San Francisco: Acme Publishing, 1952.

Thwaites, Reuben Gold, ed. *Early Western Travels, 1748–1846.* Cleveland, Ohio: Arthur H. Clark, 1905.

Todd, Bruce G. *Bones Hooks: Pioneer Negro Cowboy.* Gretna, La.: Pelican Publishing, 2005.

Tolson, Arthur L. *The Black Oklahomans: A History, 1541–1972.* New Orleans: Edwards Printing, 1974.

Tompkins, E. "Black Ahab: William T. Shorey, Whaling Master." *California Historical Quarterly* 51 (Spring 1972): 75–84.

Trivelli, Marifrances. "'I Knew a Ship from Stem to Stern': The Maritime World of Frederick Douglass." *Log of the Mystic Seaport* 46, no. 4 (1995): 98–108.

Turner, Frederick Jackson. *The Frontier in American History.* 1929. Reprint, Tucson: University of Arizona Press, 1986.

Turner, Martha Anne. *The Yellow Rose of Texas: Her Saga and Her Song.* Austin: Shoal Creek Publishers, 1976.

Utendale, Kent Alan. "Race Relations in Canada's Midwest: A Study of the Immigration, Integration, and Assimilation of Black Minority Groups." Ph.D. diss., Pacific Western University, 1985.

Utz, Scotty D. "Stepp'N Up: An African American Family Rooted in Wyoming Agriculture." Unpublished paper, University of Wyoming, 2006.

VanDeburg, William L. *Slavery and Race in American Popular Culture.* Madison: University of Wisconsin Press, 1984.

Van Deusen, John. "The Exodus of 1879." *Journal of African American History* 2, no. 1 (1936): 111–129.

Van Epps-Taylor, Betty Carol. *Oscar Micheaux . . . Dakota Homesteader, Author, Pioneer Film Maker.* Rapid City, S. Dak.: Dakota West Books, 1999.

Vestal, Stanley. *Sitting Bull: Champion of the Sioux.* Norman: University of Oklahoma Press, 1956.

Victoria Black People's Society. *Blacks in British Columbia: A Catalog of Information and Sources of Information Pertaining to Blacks in British Columbia.* Victoria, B.C.: Victoria Black People's Society, 1978.

Vinson, Ben. *Bearing Arms for His Majesty: The Free Colored Militia in Mexico.* Palo Alto, Calif.: Stanford University Press, 2001.

Walhouse, Freda. *The Influence of Minority Ethnic Groups on the Cultural Geography of Vancouver.* Vancouver: University of British Columbia Archives, Special Collections, 1961.

Walker, James W. St. G. *Canada's Ethnic Groups: The West Indians in Canada.* Publication no. 6. Ottawa: Canadian Historical Association, n.d.

Washington, Booker T. *The Story of the Negro: The Rise of the Race from Slavery.* 2 vols. New York: Peter Smith, 1909.

Washington State Library. *The Negro in the State of Washington, 1788–1969: A Bibliography of Published and of Unpublished Source Materials on the Life and Achievements of the Negro in the Evergreen State.* Rev. ed. Olympia: Washington State Library, 1970.

Wellman, Paul. *Indian Wars of the West.* New York: Indian Head Books, 1991.

Welsh, Donald H. "Pierre Wilbaux, Cattle King." *North Dakota Journal of History* 20 (1953): 5–23.

Wesley, Charles H., and Patricia Romero. *Negro Americans in the Civil War.* International Library of Negro Life and History, vol. 3. New York: Publisher's Company, 1967.

Wharfield, H. B. *10th Cavalry and Border Fights.* El Cajon, Calif.: H. B. Wharfield, 1965.

White, E. E. *Experience of a Special Indian Agent.* Norman: University of Oklahoma Press, 1965.

White, Sid, and S. E. Solberg, eds. *Peoples of Washington: Perspectives on Cultural Diversity.* Pullman: Washington State University Press, 1989.

Whitman, Sidney E. *The Troopers: An Informal History of the Plains Cavalry, 1865–1890.* New York: Hastings House, 1962.

Wight, Willard E., ed. "A Young Medical Officer's Letters from Fort Robinson and Fort Leavenworth, 1905–1907." *Nebraska History* 37 (1956): 135–47.

Willey, Austin. *The History of the Anti-slavery Cause in State and Nation.* 1860. Reprint, New York: Negro Universities Press, 1969.

Williams, George W. *History of the Negro Race in America from 1619–1880: Negroes as Slaves, Soldiers, and as Citizens.* New York: G. P. Putnam's Sons, 1883.

Williams, Gerald O. *Michael J. [A.] Healy and the Alaska Maritime Frontier, 1880–1902.* Ann Arbor: University Microfilms International, 1988.

Williams, Jennie Winona. "Allen and Winona Williams: Pioneers of Sheridan and Johnson Counties." *Annals of Wyoming* 14 (1941): 193–99.

Williams, Mildred. "An Historical Sketch of the Development of the Black Church in America and in Oakland, California." Master's thesis, Bay City Bible Institute, 1990.

Williams, Nudie Eugene. "Black Men Who Wore the 'Star.'" *Chronicles of Oklahoma* 59 (Spring 1981): 83–90.

———. "Black Political Patronage in the Western District of Arkansas, 1871–1891." *Journal of the Fort Smith Historical Society* 2 (September 1987): 5–8.

———. "Black United States Marshall in the Territory, 1875–1907." Master's thesis, Oklahoma State University, 1973.

Willis, Deborah. *Black Photographers, 1840–1940.* New York: Garland Publishers, 1985.

———. *J. P. Ball, Daguerrean and Studio Photographer.* New York: Garland Publishing, 1993.

———. *Reflections in Black: A History of Black Photographers 1840 to the Present.* New York: W. W. Norton, 2000.

Willis, Ron, and Maureen Willis. "Photography as a Tool in Genealogy." Mountain View, Calif.: Willis Photo Lab, n.d. http://freepages.genealogy.rootsweb.ancestry.com/~fgriffin/photos.txt

Wilson, Jackie Napoleon. *Hidden Witness.* New York: St. Martin's Press, 1999.

Winks, Robin W. *The Blacks in Canada: A History.* Montreal: McGill-Queen's University Press, 1971.

Woll, Allen L. *Black Musical Theatre: From Coontown to Dreamgirls.* Baton Rouge: Louisiana State University Press, 1989.

Wood, A. B. "The Coad Brothers: Panhandle Cattle Kings." *Nebraska History* 19 (1938): 28–43.

Woodson, Carter G. *The Negro in Our History.* Washington, D.C.: Associated Publishers, 1922.

Wright, Donald R. *African Americans in the Early Republic.* Arlington Heights, Ill.: Harlan Davidson, 1993.

Wyckoff, James. *John Slaughter's Way.* Garden City, N.Y.: Doubleday, 1963.

Yellin, Jean Pagan, and Cynthia D. Bond. *The Pen Is Ours: A List of Writings by and about African American Women before 1910 with Secondary Bibliography to the Present.* New York: Oxford University Press, 1991.

Zeller, Bob. *The Blue and Gray in Black and White: A History of Civil War Photography.* New York: Praeger, 2005.

Zimmer, Edward F., and Abigail B. Davis. "Recovered Views: African American Portraits, 1912–1925." *Nebraska History* 84 (2003): 59–115.

List of Collections

A WORK SUCH AS THIS could be accomplished only with the aid of dedicated, helpful, and cheerful curators and archivists. Following is a list of collections used in this text. Most are museums and libraries; some are operated by individuals. It is with great gratitude and appreciation that they are acknowledged.

Alaska State Archives. Juneau.

American Heritage Center. University of Wyoming, Laramie.

Amon Carter Museum. Fort Worth, Texas.

Anchorage Museum of History and Art. Alaska.

Anchorage Public Library. Alaska.

Arizona Historical Society. Phoenix.

Aultman, O. E. Collection. Colorado Historical Society, Denver.

Bailey, William, III. Edgemont, South Dakota.

Barry M. Goldwater Historic Photograph Collection. Arizona Historical
    Foundation, Tempe.

Bathke, Ed. Manitou Springs, Colorado.

Bishop Museum. Honolulu.

The Black American West Museum and Heritage Center. Denver.

Blakey, Ted. Yankton, South Dakota.

Boyd, Lemuel and Carolyn. Regina, Saskatchewan.

Boyd, Morris and Yvonne. Edmonton, Alberta.

California State Library. Sacramento.

Caribbean Association of Manitoba. Canada.

Casper College. Casper, Wyoming.

Church of Jesus Christ of Latter-day Saints Historical Department. Salt Lake City.

Cincinnati Art Museum. Cincinnati.

City of Oakland. California.

City of Sacramento Archives. California.

City of Vancouver Archives. British Columbia.

Coe Library, Reference Section. University of Wyoming, Laramie.

Collins Street Bakery. Corsicana, Texas.

Colorado Historical Society. Denver.

Denver Public Library. Western History Collection. Denver.

Fort Huachuca, Arizona.

Fort Robinson State Park. Crawford, Nebraska.

Fort Sill Museum. Oklahoma.

Fort Verde State Park. Arizona.

Gilcrease Museum. Tulsa, Oklahoma.

Gillespie, W. Gordon. Laramie, Wyoming.

Glenbow Museum. Calgary, Alberta.

Grant City Museum. Canyon City, Oregon.

Graves, R. W. Collection. Chadron State University Library, Nebraska.

Great Plains Black Museum. Omaha, Nebraska.

Hallmark Photographic Collection at the Nelson-Atkins Museum of Art. Kansas City,
      Missouri.

Hawaii State Archives. Honolulu.

Hayes, Ralph. Seattle.

Haynes Foundation Collection. Montana Historical Society, Helena.

Idaho State Historical Society. Boise.

Institute of Texan Cultures. San Antonio.

John Slaughter Ranch and Harvey Finks, curator and manager, Arizona.

John Slaughter State Park. Arizona.

Kansas State Historical Society. Topeka.

Kercherval, Beatrice. Edgemont, South Dakota.

LaFrantz Collection. American Heritage Center, University of Wyoming, Laramie.

Lahaina Whaling Museum and Rick Ralston. Hawaii.

Latah County Historical Society. Moscow, Idaho.

Lewis County Historical Museum. Chehalis, Washington.

Library of Congress. Washington, D.C.

Little Big Horn National Monument. Crow Agency, Montana.

Marion/Lee County Historical Society Museum. Missouri.

Matthews, Miriam Collection. California African-American Museum, Los Angeles.

Mission House Museum Library. Honolulu.

Montana State Historical Society. Helena.

Moorland-Spingarn Research Collection. Howard University. Washington, D.C.

Museum of New Mexico. Santa Fe.

Mystic Seaport Museum. Connecticut.

National Archives. Washington, D.C.

National Park Service. Anchorage.

Nebraska State Historical Society. Lincoln.

Nevada State Historical Society. Reno.

Nicholson, J. Guthrie, Jr. Collection. American Heritage Center, University of
Wyoming, Laramie.

North Dakota State Historical Society. Bismarck.

Northern California Center for Afro-American History Museum. Oakland.

Oregon Historical Society. Portland.

Palmquist, Peter. Arvata, California.

Perue, Dick, Historical Photos. Saratoga, Wyoming.

Pingenot, Ben E. Collection. Brackettville, Texas.

Providence Public Library Archives. Rhode Island.

Raleigh Township Memorial Museum. North Buxton, Ontario.

Rasmussen Collection. University of Alaska Archives, Fairbanks.

Roslyn Museum. Roslyn, Washington.

San Francisco Public Library. San Francisco, California.

Saskatchewan Provincial Archives. Regina.

Savery Museum. Savery, Wyoming.

Sharlott Hall Museum. Prescott, Arizona.

Smithsonian Institute. Washington, D.C.

South Dakota State Historical Society. Pierre.

Spokane Northwest Black Pioneers. Washington.

Spokane Public Library. Washington.

Stepp-Evans, Geraldine. Denver.

Sweetwater County Library. Green River, Wyoming.

Teton County Historical Society. Jackson, Wyoming.

Thermopolis Museum. Wyoming.

Tulia Museum. Texas.

Tuskegee University Archives. Alabama.

University of Nevada. Reno.

University of North Dakota. Grand Forks.

University of Washington Special Collections. Seattle.

University of Wyoming Library, Reference Section. Laramie.

Ursuline Centre. Great Falls, Montana.

U.S. Geological Survey Photographic Archives. Denver.

Utendale, Kent. Vancouver, British Columbia.

Webber, William Hallam. Rockville, Maryland.

Western Kentucky State University Archives. Bowling Green.

White House Collection. Washington, D.C.

Woolarock State Parks. Oklahoma. [Woolaroc Museum and Wildlife Preserve Collection]

Wyoming State Museum and Archive. Cheyenne.

XIT Museum. Dalhart, Texas.

Yellowstone National Park Archives. Mammoth, Wyoming.

Index